T0063453

Forward

Forward

HOW TO GET UNSTUCK AND BECOME UNSTOPPABLE

BOGDAN KIPKO

WestBow Press
P R E S S
A DIVISION OF THOMAS NELSON

Share, tweet and post any quotes from the book using the following hashtag: #forwardbook

WestBow Press books may be ordered through booksellers or by contacting:

WestBow Press
A Division of Thomas Nelson
1663 Liberty Drive
Bloomington, IN 47403
www.westbowpress.com
1 (866) 928-1240

Cover design by kleverkatdesign.com.

ISBN: 978-1-4908-1324-0 (sc)
ISBN: 978-1-4908-1325-7 (e)

Library of Congress Control Number: 2013918940

Printed in the United States of America.

WestBow Press rev. date: 11/04/2013

This book is dedicated to my local church where I am privileged to be one of the pastors. Thank you for letting me be a part of your journey with Jesus.

CONTENTS

INTRODUCTION

"Now to him who is able to do far more abundantly than
all that we ask or think, according to the power at work
within us, to him be glory in the church and in Christ
Jesus throughout all generations, forever and ever."
(Ephesians 3:20-21)

*J*esus is able to do through us, far more than imagined by us. Unfortunately, we are far too easily amused, far too easily pleased and all too quickly submit to mediocrity in every single part of our life. We stop striving for more, stop praying for bigger and stop delivering excellence. It is far easier to just live a comfortable life and wait until retirement occurs. Someone else can chase the dream, someone else can change the world, someone else can influence people, someone else can move forward, someone else can become unstuck while becoming unstoppable—I can just sleep in while the rest of the world is wide awake.

The last ten years have been an absolute whirlwind for my wife and I. We both lost our beloved dads to cancer. I moved to a new state, started work at a new company, assimilated to a new church and started and finished my graduate degree in seminary. This was happening while I was working full time in the corporate world and in the church. We both went through peaks and valleys in every single sphere of our life. We experienced our fair share of difficulties and arguments as a brand new couple, learning to live together as a married couple. We went through a difficult time in ministry that nearly left us depleted and emptied, both physically and spiritually. There were many times when it seemed like we were completely stuck with no way out. But Jesus does not save you from every storm, because He wants to save you through the storm. If it were not for the gospel of Jesus Christ that was intricately interwoven into the fabric of our lives, I do not want to know where we would be today. So even though getting stuck was a part of my life, it does not define my life. Only Jesus can offer you the hope that a multitude of other counterfeit gods are offering you today.

So if you are like me, you have experienced a scenario of being stuck in a situation that makes it seemingly impossible to become unstoppable. But here is the crazy part: God created you to live, fully alive. He created you to step into the script that has already been written. The epic narrative where Jesus is the hero and you are the ultimate image of that Hero. I hear people complain all the time that they don't have enough resources to fulfill their dream. That they don't have enough time to work on their craft. That they don't have enough money to fund their project. Guess who has all of that? God. God has all the resources in the world. God has all the time in the world. God has all the money in the world. What would your life look like when you dangerously surrender as a saint into the hands of a happy God? The same God who can move mountains, can do even greater miracles in your life.

The greatest danger that we face in life is not doing bad things but rather not doing enough good things. The greatest tragedy you can encounter in life is not ruining it but rather wasting it. So what kind of legacy will you create? What kind of legacy are you creating? What are you doing right now, to make the biggest impact for Jesus' fame and in Jesus name? This is the question that you need to answer. Because a life lived for self without the realization of God's dreams for you is a wasted life. And to come to a sober realization of this reality on your last day, would be an irreversible catastrophe.

I believe that God created us for far more than we are actually engaged in. We are like people who have a jet-pack strapped onto our back, but fail to engage the start button. The same power that gives dead men life is the same power that lives in us. The same power that raised the brutally murdered Messiah back to life as Lord and King over all is the same power that lives in all those who declare Jesus as Lord over their life.

But before God will use you greatly, He will wound you deeply. Before God will do a great work through you, He wants to first do a great work in you. Before you will turn the world upside down around you, God wants to turn the world upside down, inside of you. Because if you can't lead yourself, you won't be able to lead other people.

This is a book about engaging in a brutally honest assessment of your life, to see the condition of your life. This is a book about seeing who you are and *Whose* you are. This is a book about realizing the density of your depravity and the beauty of Jesus, who saves you and sustains you.

This is a book written for different looking sinners, in need of the same looking Cross. This is a book written by an author who has failed miserably, but has been saved gloriously. This is a book to give you hope that even though your sin may be deep, Jesus' love for you is deeper still. This is a book that will tell you on every page, that if you have breath in your lungs, God has a plan for your life. A plan that is far better, bigger and immeasurably more than anything you have ever imagined. It is yours for the taking.

I truly believe that Jesus wants His followers to be the most influential, the most optimistic, the most enthusiastic, the most unstuck, the most unstoppable and the most forward of all people that populate this planet. He wants us to be movement makers, continent shakers and earth axis adjusters.

So here we go. Together, we are going to move forward. Jesus wants you to become unstuck, so that you can become unstoppable. In order for you to do that, I am deeply convinced that there are four areas of your life that need to be closely examined and painfully scrutinized. Without these four spheres of your life, functioning in a forward motion, I don't see how you can get unstuck to become unstoppable.

As you read this book, contemplate with vulnerability and openness about the true condition of your heart, in relation to the One who created that heart. Ask God to reveal to you the hidden areas in your life, so that His merciful light can flood you with grace and peace. Because it is not about your performance in these four areas of your life, but rather Jesus' performance in every sphere of your life. It is not about how well you do this but rather how well it has already been done, by the One who has conquered and won you, personally.

My prayerful and passionate desire is that as you consume the content in this book, your love for Jesus would become more passionate, your love for people would become more visible and your imaging of Jesus would be absolutely undeniable, to the watching world in need of radical redemption. We are not the heroes of our story but rather Jesus is the Hero of this great story we call life. Today is the day when you will start living a life with faith that matches the size of the God who gave you that faith in the first place. Today is the day when you get unstuck and become unstoppable. You have one life to live. Let's go. *Forward*.

Part One

CONNECT WITH GOD

"We can all co-exist, but we will not all co-end up in heaven. Jesus is the way."

Chapter 1

THE FORWARD MANIFESTO

Keep a close watch on yourself and on the
teaching. Persist in this, for by so doing you
will save both yourself and your hearers.
(1 Tim. 4:16)

*"If you want to change the way you live your life,
you must move forward with your life."*

I am convinced more than ever before that it will be
literally impossible to make a long-lasting impact upon
people in your life without these five critical commitments.
If you publicly confess that Jesus is your Lord, I personally do
not see how these things would not be a regular rhythm of
your life.

3

We must put in grace-fueled effort to intentionally and consistently pursue these critical commitments, if we are to demonstrate an authentic Christianity:

1. **Preach What You Practice.** Respect is received when what you say is backed up with how you live. Many people want to say something but few have something to say. Titles do not nearly carry as much authority as a life lived under authority. Your life and doctrine must be two lanes upon the highway of your life, headed in the same direction. We must be able to sit under our own teaching and our own advice. If I am pointing out a sin in someone's life, I should be bold enough to display humility when someone is doing the same to me. As sinful human beings, we will fail at preaching what we practice. But this should be the exception in our life, not the norm for our life.

2. **Confess Your Struggles.** I recently witnessed something publicly that I have seldom seen from leaders. It was a confession that they lie a lot. Did that person lose credibility in my eyes? Not at all. Quite the opposite. Willing to admit that you are not ok and are in a desperate need of Jesus every waking moment—is a sign that you are preaching what you practice. Should you air out your less than stellar linen for all to discuss? No. But sporadically stating that you too have not yet arrived, keeps you humble and gives listeners hope. The very fact that you confess to others, closes the gap between your public life and your private life. The two should not have a false dichotomy. Vulnerability is the new currency. The individual who has built an impenetrable fortress displaying the fortitude of

their morality is first and foremost deceiving themselves personally and leading astray others, corporately. Confess your sins to one another so that the great Physician, can help and heal. If we don't demonstrate at least a small level of vulnerability, we run the risk of displaying dishonesty which leads to hypocrisy. The good news of the gospel is that hypocrites are welcome because Christ's perfection carries our imperfection.

3. **Seek Out Mentors.** If no one is speaking in to your life, pressing Christ into your life or relaying to you the blind spots of your life—you will make a wreck of your life. Someone other than *you* needs to help *you*. Someone needs to come alongside of you and help you examine your thoughts, motivations, behaviors and ambitions. Instead of waiting for someone to mentor us, we need to seek out mentors and request that they provide mentoring to us. Do not seek mentors only during times of catastrophe or crisis. Seek out mentors when everything is going well. A mentor can uncover your areas of weakness and potentially save you from heartache and bad decision-making. A mentor can catapult your leadership and influence at an exponential rate. Mentors help you get further, faster—wherever your final destination may be. Yes, Jesus is our ultimate mentor. Godly men and women who love Jesus are the perfect candidates to come in to your life and mentor you during your life. I personally do not want to imagine where I would be without mentors in my life. Have they helped me arrive? Absolutely not. They are just helping me along the road of life so that I hit less speed bumps, avoid traffic and stay within the proverbial speed limit.

4. **Remain Approachable.** I love the concept of 360 degree coaching. It means I welcome it from anyone. I do not want to be a puffed-up general, barking out orders and being defensive when addressed with advice. I want to serve with humility, accept criticism without activating my inner lawyer and remain approachable. Invite people to point out places in your life where you demonstrate less than stellar Christianity. If God knows what you think, what you have done, what you will do and what you want to do—then why fear what people will think about you? If all you do is focus on your religious performance, you have no room to celebrate the spiritual maturity of other people in your life. Remain approachable. Remain teachable. Contrary to personal opinion, you do not know everything.

5. **Cultivate Candid Community.** Invite people into your life, so that they can speak life into you. Cultivate friendships within your community, at the expense of personal comfort. Nothing will propel you into a deeper spiritual maturity than being a part of a community and nothing will propel you into a false sense of confidence about your level of sinfulness than being apart from a community. A community has an ability to speak into your life with Biblical clarity and accuracy—in a way in which you are unable to, personally.

You can make a great impression at a distance but you will only make a great impact up close.

People around you will not be shaped by your knowledge or talent or skill. They will be shaped by the heart motivation that personally drives your actions. The behavior you demonstrate will be the behavior that is imitated. What you imitate, you will ultimately replicate. A pursuit of unity and humility in a community can become our greatest and most potent testimony.

Often, the only Jesus a person will ever see is the one you are demonstrating. Sometimes, the only Bible people will read, is the life you lead. I believe that at the most basic level, when a person looks at a follower of Christ, all they want to see is Jesus.

These five commitments are not reserved for those who are in ministry or leadership. These commitments are integral to any follower of Jesus. If we are to be the letter of Christ to the watching world, we must write well the message that will be read by many.

This is the *Forward* Manifesto.

Chapter 2

IT'S NOT ABOUT YOU

And the city has no need of sun or moon to shine on it, for
the glory of God gives it light, and its lamp is the Lamb.
(Rev. 21:23)

*"Our life must be shaped by an eagerness to display God's
glory, instead of wanting others to see our glory."*

We often think that God is all about us. That God's
mission revolves around us. We look at the world
surrounding us and then we look at ourselves. We then use our
cultural lens to conclude from that position specifically what
God is all about. And here is the answer we come up with:

God's mission is about *us*
God's mission is about *me*
We are conditioned to think much of *me*.

The reason that everything exists is so that God might:

Save me
Rescue me
Replicate me
Create more prototypes who are exactly like me

Of course the following is true:

God loves us
God saves us
God cares for us
God shepherds us
God provides for us
God shields us
God protects us

Functioning from this position, we begin to think that we are actually *the* point. We begin to think that *we* are the center of the universe. That everything exists, including both people and God to please us, serve us, be of service to us and submit to us. We begin to think that we are what God is after.

Let me be clear:

God *is* for us
God *does* love us
God *does* provide for us
God *is* a shield for us
God *is* a protector for us

But—there is a motivation behind all of these items that God is inevitably all about.

Here it is:

God Cares More About His Glory Than Your Story

The motivation of God behind all of these positive items that we think are all about *us*, goes well *beyond* us.

I want to look at a very familiar passage with you that substantiates this statement. You most likely have memorized this verse when you were a young child, going to Sunday School. You most likely can still recite this verse if prompted today. Even if you do not have a church background, there is no doubt that you have come across this verse.

Psalm 23:1-3:

The LORD is my shepherd; I shall not want. He makes me lie down in green pastures. He leads me beside still waters. He restores my soul. He leads me in paths of righteousness for his name's sake.

When you look at these verses, you can see all of the things that God is doing for us:

He is shepherding us
He is making sure we are not in a dire need of anything
He desires for us to be taken care of
He gives us peace and tranquility to rest beside still waters
He restores our anxious soul

He prepares for us paths that have been first traveled on and cleared for our sake

But, please look at verse three along with me. What does it say? *He restores my soul. He leads me in paths of righteousness*—for what? The absolute root of all of God's motivation to do all of the above great things that we experience is found at the end of verse three.

Here it is:
for his name's sake.

Why does God love you? Why does God pursue you? Why does God shepherd you? What is it for? What is the primary motivation behind all of the things that God does for us?

It is for His name's sake!

Why does God save us?
Why does God send His Son Jesus Christ to die a brutal death on a cross?
Why is God restoring our anxious soul?
Why is God giving us peace and tranquility during tumultuous times?
Why does He make sure we are taken care of?
Why does He provide for us?
Why does He make sure we are not in need of anything?

It is not because of *you*. It is not because of *me*. We are *not* the point. The whole reason God does any and all of this—is **for his name's sake.**

It is for the praise of **His** glorious grace.

It is for the praise of **His** glorious name.

It is for the exaltation of who **He** is.

It is for the perpetual worship of **Him** for who **He** is and what **He** has done for us, not because of us, but despite us for **Himself**.

This truth needs to encourage us, not distress us. This truth that *God cares more about His glory than your story* must be the *best* news we have ever heard. Why? Because we exist to give glory to God. We exist to perpetually worship our Creator. We exist to be governed by God's principles for our life because they were created for our joy.

This is precisely the reason why Jesus came to die on the cross. There on the cross of Calvary, the immeasurable glory of God was put on full display for the whole world to see. There on the cross of Calvary, in a magnificent display of glory and power, the inestimable goodness of God was displayed before the whole world.

Jesus absorbed the wrath of God in place of us so that once we are quickened by the Holy Spirit, we can spend our entire life time giving glory to God who saved us for Himself.

This is the very epicenter of the gospel. God is the gospel! The gospel is God coming to earth as a human to save humans. For what purpose? To save humans for *Himself* through his son Jesus Christ. This is why the glory of God and our rendering of glory to Him is infinitely more important than our story. God is not about *you*. He is about *His* glory. But your story is a great display of His glory.

Chapter 3

A DREAM CRUSHED

For we are his workmanship, created in Christ
Jesus for good works, which God prepared
beforehand, that we should walk in them.
(Eph. 2:10)

"God wants to give you what you need,
not necessarily what you want."

When I was a teenager, I was throughly obsessed with becoming a stock broker. Ever since I watched the movie *Boiler Room*, I could not get this idea out of my head. I wanted to work in a high rise building in New York City. I wanted to live the exciting and jagged edge lifestyle of a stock broker.

At that early stage of my adult life, I thought this would be the absolute best thing that could happen to me. I shared this dream with my parents. I shared this dream with those close to me. My mind was locked in on this and I wanted it more than anything else.

But as life progressed, this dream became elusive. Not a single event in my life was going the way of this dream. Instead of trading stocks, I was always writing essays. Instead of analyzing the market, I was reading different books and leading Bible studies. I slowly started realizing that this was not something that was going to happen in my life. At first, I was devastated. It seemed so real when watching the movie. It seemed so real when I would day dream about it, sitting in my small cubicle, making over 100 phone calls per hour, surrounded by drug addicts and semi-homeless people who also called this call center their preferred employer.

We all have goals, dreams and aspirations. We all have things that our mind effortlessly drifts toward when it is on idle mode. There is something right now in your life that is your exclusive motivation to continue forward. There is something that you obsessively think about. There is something that determines your mood, alters your behavior and directs your life choices. Whatever that thing is, the power it produces is unmatched by anything else. Only you know what it is. You might not have even shared it with anyone. Some people connected to you can only assume what it is.

What if I was to tell you that there is a chance that it might never happen? Your dream. Your hope. Your pursuit. Your aspiration. What if there was a chance that it will never come to pass. It will remain in an ethereal sphere never reaching tangible reality. Some years ago, this happened to me. I was wrecked and devastated.

As I got more involved in church and ministry, I realized that God actually knew what He was doing in my life. As my call to ministry was more robustly amplified, I understood what was happening:

God took my dream, blew it up into small pieces and destroyed the evidence. He then placed in that empty space something that was conceived not by humanity but rather by divinity.

But the transition process was painful. It is never pleasurable to have your dream taken from you and shattered before your very eyes.

What will you do if your dreams do not come true?

Chapter 4

JESUS IS THE BETTER DREAM

And he [Jesus] is before all things, and
in him all things hold together.
(Col. 1:17)

"The God who gave you life knows exactly how to sustain your life."

*M*ost people have a few set hopes and dreams for their life. Most young people want to get married, start a family, secure a position in society and remain influential, culturally.

Beginning with this basic framework, two streams emerge: One is content with accomplishing basic primal instincts. This first stream conducts life in a relatively civil manner. The other stream is more ambitious and wishes to impact the world in which they reside. Here is the potential disaster that this second group will face:

Suppose that you have a dream. This is a dream that you just can't release from your mind. It drives you. It might even control you. You might be obsessed over it. This is not necessarily a bad thing. Your dream is most likely noble in character. You want to make money to tithe regularly. You want your ministry to impact more than one hundred people. You want to be loved and appreciated by your community. You want to get married and have an "x" amount of kids. You want to maintain a certain lifestyle level. You want to make a historical impact and leave a great legacy.

There can be various ways in which the above will come to pass in your life. But what if I told you that there is a chance that your dream will not come true? What if I told you that there might be a change of direction in your future. What if I told you that whatever you concocted in your mind does not necessarily fit into your life story? Would you still be content in life? Would you still be satisfied? What would your reaction be?

What if I told you that God intentionally wants to take your dream and smash it into a million pieces? What if I said that the dream you have in your mind is mediocre compared to what God has prepared for you. How would you react if God came to you directly to take that dream out of your hand to give it to someone else? What if the dream you had percolating in your mind for over two decades was meant for someone else to accomplish?

David was God's chosen King over Israel. God took him from the pasture and placed him in a palace (1 Chr. 17:7). God took away his shabby shepherd clothing and gave him a wardrobe reserved for royalty. God loved David so much that the Bible says he was a man after God's own heart (1 Sam. 13:14). David was also a dreamer. He had a dream to build a huge temple for the God that He loved.

David's dream was noble in character. David was ashamed that his residence was a house of cedar and the ark of the covenant remained under a tent (1 Chr. 17:1). This dream of David kept him awake at night. Every breathing moment of his existence was preoccupied with this dream. He wanted it so badly. He justified in his mind the validity of this dream. He even shared his dream with other people. His dream was contagious. He had no problem in gathering a huge team to accomplish this feat. He had the resources. He had the energy. He had the charisma. He had the talent. He had the money. He had the right knowledge. Even his heart was supposedly in the right place. There was absolutely no logical reason why his dream would not come to pass.

What happened next was a situation ripe for complete and utter personal and professional meltdown.

Nathan the Prophet was assigned to be the bearer of the bad news. He was carrying the dream of David in a crystal vase. Moments later, this fragile vase of a dream would be shattered right before the watching eyes of David.

Here is what the Lord wanted to say to David:

It is not *you* who will build me a house to dwell in (1 Chr. 17:4).

Can you allow these words to sink in for a few seconds? This moment reminds me of the deafening silence right after a catastrophe occurs. You see the people around you, gripped by the reality and stunned by silence. There is a thick smoke in the air. Debris and collateral damage begin to find its way back to the ground. In a dazed stupor, you find your balance and begin to look around you. What. just. happened.

As you begin to regain a sense of consciousness, God continues to speak.

Here is what He says to David: *Instead of you building me a house to dwell in, here is what is going to happen. I will build you a house. A house that is not temporal or physical but eternal and perpetual* (1 Chr. 17:10-15).

Did you see what just happened? Did you catch it?

God blew up David's dream and replaced it with His own.

He says, *David—I love you and I want what is best for you—I want your dreams to come true—But you need to realize that the dreams that will come true are the ones that I implanted into you! These are divine dreams that inevitably will bring me the glory I desire and rightfully deserve!*

Instead of David building God a house, God promises to build David a house. A kingdom that will be established not temporarily but eternally.

Your reaction to the shattered dream will reveal the true condition of your heart. God wants you to delight in Him so that He would grant you the desires of your heart. But He wants to do it in a way that brings Him maximum glory. God wants to take our dreams, detonate a bomb that will shatter them to pieces, and in the middle of that wreckage, He wants to implant something that even our wildest imagination could not come up with.

Here is what David's reaction was: He began to worship God. He began to exalt God. He began to thank God. David affirms God's will in His life. David says: *There is none like you, O LORD, and there is no God besides you* (1 Chr. 17:16-27).

Jesus is our greater dream. Whatever dream we have, whatever ambition we carry, Jesus is greater. Jesus is greater than any dream that I have. Jesus is better than any goal that I set.

If this is our mindset, then we will not have to deal with collateral damage when our dream is shattered before our eyes. If we can only understand this concept, our entire life would be radically altered. Our perspective on things that happen in our life would look much different. We would be much calmer. We would experience far less anxiety.

What matters is not that your dream is fulfilled but that your hope is firmly placed in Jesus and Jesus alone.

Your dreams cannot take the place of Jesus. Your dreams unmistakably fall short of those that Jesus has to offer.

God wants to shatter your dreams not because He wants to take away your joy. God wants to shatter your dreams because they are too small, too mediocre and too narrow. God wants you to understand that His Son Jesus Christ, whom He sent to earth to die on the cross in your place—is your greater and better dream.

Chapter 5

THE BIGGEST DANGER
FOR CHRISTIANS

In the same way, let your light shine before others,
so that they may see your good works and give
glory to your Father who is in heaven.
(Matt. 5:16)

*"The tragedy in our life won't be doing many bad
things but rather not doing enough good things."*

The biggest danger that most Christians will face won't
be:

Sinning too much, because first of all, you can't out sin God.
Ultimately, God knows you inside and out, knows what you
are thinking, doing and feeling. Nothing you do will ever
surprise Him.

Doing too many bad things. You don't do bad things, you were born bad. You are born locked into a trespass zone. None of your phenomenal efforts will get you out of it. The phenomenal effort of Jesus is your only hope.

Ruining your life, because of bad decisions. The worst decision ever made has already been paid for and resolved. No matter how many bad decisions you make, Jesus' sacrifice for you on the cross is sufficient to cover all of them.

The biggest danger most Christians will face in their life won't be *ruining* their lives but rather *wasting* their lives.

The great tragedy for many of us will not be doing a lot of bad things but rather not doing enough good things. Not living life, awake to the reality of the heavy price that was paid for our life. Not living a life, in reverential amazement of a holy God who saves hell-bound sinners.

We were not created just to say a prayer, just to get baptized, just to say the right phrases, just to get married and settle in, just to exist in a church for multiple decades and then fade out into eternity. Those are all great things, but they are not the main things.

Here are four ways we are wasting our life, the one shot we get at making an eternal impact, because of Jesus' impact:

1. **Mindless Entertainment.** We are a culture that is getting entertained to death. We have nine devices that we use at

any singular moment. Streaming, downloading, updating, uploading, clicking, buzzing, switching, fast-forwarding, queueing, deciding. The problem with our culture is not a lack of information but an abundance of it. It's like we are constantly drinking from a fire hydrant.

Google has destroyed our capacity to think. Pinterest has destroyed our creativity. Instagram made everyone a professional food photographer. And now, some electronic glasses will gouge the last bit of imagination we could have produced on our own.

Instead of turning to real people, we turn on the television, so that it would keep us company. We watch the news and have been tricked by the news-casters to think that the words "*and now*," "*breaking*," and "*this just in*," are actually proclamations of something we won't be able to breathe without, if we don't watch it. News has become entertainment in and of itself. It gives us something to talk about, but cannot lead to any meaningful action.

2. **Doing the same thing every day and expecting a different result.** I was speaking with a friend recently who said that he tried to wake up early for a week and quit trying after that. When I asked how come, he said that it was way too early and way to difficult. If you are used to waking up at the crack of 12pm, you won't wake up at 5am immediately. Incremental change is what is going to take, to make that happen. Start with waking up at least thirty minutes before your usual slumber session.

3. **Not investing time into people.** We think that we
can go about our business, not invest in our relationships
with our spouse, our friends or our community group—
and then expect everyone to be supremely interested in
who you are as a person. It just does not happen that way.
Everything you do in life, has to have strategic intention
about it. Anything worth doing, is worth doing well. Jesus
was intent on accomplishing the will of His Father, while
here on earth. He had laser focus. Do you? Do I? Are you
making a great investment with your life or are you wasting
your life?

4. **Settling down and checking out.** A lot of people get
married and immediately drop out of the church, drop out
of a community group and start focusing on their own small
tribe, all the while neglecting the Tribe of Christ. Why
does this happen? Because somewhere along the way, they
were fed a lie that this is all to life. I remember how some
adults used to come up to me and say that I reminded them
of how they were when they were young, full of energy and
charisma, ready to change the world. My question is—how
is that particular approach to life locked in to a particular
age group?

If you have breath in your lungs, God has a plan for your life.
A plan that is far better, bigger and immeasurably more than
anything you have ever imagined. Jesus is able to do far more
abundantly than all that we ask or think, according to the
power at work within us.

Part Two

COMMUNE WITH OTHERS

"A great relationship is formed, not found."

Chapter 6

RECKLESS LOVE

but God shows his love for us in that while
we were still sinners, Christ died for us.
(Rom. 5:8)

"True love does not demand reciprocation"

I was sitting on the seventh floor of an outside patio in
a restaurant overlooking the downtown of an influential
city. The weather was phenomenal, the food was going to be
delicious and my beautiful wife was attentively listening to my
latest idea. With deep anticipation, I was perusing through the
menu, deciding my destiny. I noticed that each page that listed
menu items had another page that listed various advertisements.
One in particular caught my attention.

It was an invitation to come out for an event which was all about *equality, love* and *community*. As I looked at the fine print, I quickly realized this was not an invitation to a community group, hosted by a local church. It was something completely different. The words were attractive—but they were not being used in the way in which they were intended originally.

Before my wife and I were married, we made a mutual decision. We decided that we were not going to say *"I love you,"* to one another, until the day that I proposed to her. We wanted our words to have weight, to have meaning, to make an impact. Especially when we are talking about the word *love*. Did I not love her during the time I was intentionally pursuing her? Of course I did! But during our two and one half year courtship, I never once told her that I love her. I wanted to save these words for the most special of occasions.

The word *love* has been completely re-defined and is always being mis-used. The culture we live in has completely re-defined many words that we use. Words that carried weight and meaning before, now are left limp and completely mis-used. Jesus says that out of the abundance of our heart, the mouth speaks. The Apostle Paul says that God has chosen word-gifts and word-offices to build up the church. God even created the world through words. God regenerates through His word. We are called to meditate on the words of God and write them on the tablet of our heart.

I hear people loving all sorts of things. People *love* jelly-beans. People *love* the individual who went to do a Starbucks run for the office. This word is used flippantly and can address any sort of triviality. Is it bad to love all those things? No. But saying that you *"love,"* everything dilutes the actual weight of this particular word.

Jesus said that we must love one another as He has loved us.

Jesus said that the greatest love that can be demonstrated is when you lay down your life for your friends.

Biblical love loves you at your worst.

When you do not have it all together. When you have not been insta-grammed and photoshopped.

Biblical love continues where human love stops. Biblical love pursues when human love gets exhausted. Biblical love looks at a person not as humans do, but as God does—through the filter of Jesus.

A gospel type of love says *"I have seen you at your lowest point and I still love you."*

Jesus centered love says *"You are not perfect, but Jesus is and my love for you is perfected by Him."*

Cultural love says *"I will continue to love you so long as you fulfill my requests and satisfy my desires."*

Biblical love says *"I will continue to love you even if you do not fulfill my requests or satisfy my desires—because ultimately—only Jesus can do both, perfectly and completely."*

Cultural loves says "*I will love you so long as you agree with my plan and don't derail it.*"

Biblical love says "*I will love you even if you do not agree with me and are not on board with the plan that I have.*"

Biblical love says: "*I do not have to always agree with you, to be friends with you.*"

Relationships can often be messy, difficult, broken, in need of repair, almost beyond hope and at times, seemingly irreconcilable. But every single time you pick up the pieces, begin the painful process of reconciliation, repair that which is broken and make a shattered friendship completely whole again—you are imaging and displaying to the watching world that which Jesus has done for you personally.

So what do you do when that love is not evident in your relationships, with the people in your life?

The Apostle Paul's letter to the Romans reaches its crescendo in chapter five where he pens these words full of resolve and relief:

Therefore, since we have been justified by faith, we have peace with God through our Lord Jesus Christ (Rom. 5:1).

When we are granted the gift of faith—we are ushered into a territory of grace where Jesus is King and Redeemer. This means that we are no longer under the wrath of God but rather glad recipients of His grace. This means that as we live out our lives in pursuit of Christ-likeness—we image Jesus to the watching world. We practically do this by pursuing and restoring broken relationships—if at all possible (Rom. 12:18). We become reconciliatory ambassadors in every single part of our life.

The collective pattern of our choices, regardless of magnitude—amplify the primary source that shapes our character. If we are to have the character of Christ—we must be first to pursue one another in restoring that which is broken or in need of repair.

Here are ten reasons why it is imperative for us to pursue and restore a broken relationship:

1. **We reconcile with others because Jesus first reconciles us to God.** When we pursue a broken relationship, our focus should be on the other person and what we need to do—instead of what they did and what they need to do to make it right. This principle of reaping and sowing creates reciprocity in a relationship.

2. **We restore relationships because Jesus first restored our broken relationship with God.** We were at one time foes of God but Jesus makes us friends with God. The process of restoration can be painful and difficult—but so was the cross for Jesus and He still actively obeyed His Father to accomplish the most epic act of love that history has ever seen, or will see.

3. **We pursue peace with others because Jesus first created peace between us and God.** We become planters of peace in our relationships when we intentionally

function from a peace-centered perspective. We are peace-makers because we worship the greater Peace-maker. The Bible promises that those who sow in peace reap a harvest of righteousness (Js. 3:18). This is exactly what Jesus did—by peacefully submitting to the will of His Father—going to the cross—and providing us with His righteousness.

4. **We repair our friendships with others because Jesus first repaired our broken relationship with God.** A strong friendship is founded upon a firm foundation—upon a cornerstone—upon Jesus Christ. That means that my friendship is first not because of some sort of trivial affinity but because of the Trinity.

5. **We pick up the shattered pieces and create a beautiful display of God's glory because Jesus first took our divided heart and made it complete again.** We were created by a Creator God to create all things new. This means that we bring restorative creativity into our lives by taking something broken and with Jesus' interference, make it whole again.

6. **We love others because Jesus first loved us.** We do not wait to be loved to extend love to others. We do not wait to feel like loving to start loving.

7. **We do not wait for someone else to initiate reconciliation with us** first but rather pursue the other person out of the conviction that Jesus first pursued us when we were running from Him.

8. **We do not ever neglect or forget because Jesus promised to never leave us nor forsake us.**

9. **We extend grace first and foremost because Jesus extends grace to us.**

10. **We pursue the relationship, no matter the cost, because Jesus too counted the cost** and found us valuable enough to give His life—so that we could gain a life

Instead of culture re-defining for us what love is, we must influence the culture by showing it what love does.

Love is a verb.

You have one life to show as much of it as possible to the watching world.

Chapter 7

SOUL MATE CENTRAL

Therefore a man shall leave his father and mother and
hold fast to his wife, and the two shall become one
flesh.' So they are no longer two but one flesh. What
therefore God has joined together, let not man separate.
(Mark 10:7-9)

*"You don't become a better spouse be getting married.
You become a better spouse by staying married."*

7 believe that the concept of having a *"soul-mate,"* is
Biblical. The person you marry *IS* your soul-mate. The
Bible is very clear about that: Mark 10:7-9; Eph. 5:22-33. Your
spouse will be your soul-mate. Your spouse *IS* the standard of
beauty for you. Your spouse *IS* the most beautiful and awe-
inspiring person in your life. If you swerve from this mentality,
your marriage may experience a dangerous derailment.

Is it possible to marry the wrong person? The Bible says if we trust in God with all of our heart and lean not on our own understanding, acknowledging Him in everything—He promises to make our "paths straight" (Prov. 3:5-6). This statement is *prescriptive*, not *prophetic*. The Bible teaches us *how* to live our life but it does not force upon us the *way* we live our life. If you are not trusting God, not leaning in to His understanding and heavily relying upon yours—then the implication of the text underscores the foolish nature of *your* decisions—not God's. You can take a wrong turn and go in the wrong direction, including marrying the wrong person. It is possible—in a time of disobedience to God's commandments to marry the wrong person—BUT—even in such a case—God is still *sovereign*, God is *still* in control and God still would like for your marriage to thrive and flourish. Even if a marriage was not the desire of God, it does not mean that it was not in the plan of God. The Bible teaches us that God hates divorce (Mal. 2:16). As humans created in God's image, we *too* must hate what God hates.

This is how we image the living gospel to the watching world. By being perpetual worshipers in all spheres of life—including the married life.

Sometimes, people say the following:

"I married the wrong person and will not truly be happy until I find my true soul-mate."

Here are two things that are wrong with this statement:

1. **You are claiming that the decision made in your life is being over-ridden by God's will for your life.** Even though you might not have made the right decision—this does not mean that God cannot use this decision for His glory. There is no way that you personally can destroy a decision made by God for your life, specifically.

2. **You are claiming that God is not powerful enough, potent enough or effective enough to take a shattered relationship and make it whole again.** You are also practicing temporary atheism, where you believe the gospel of Jesus *confessionally*, but do not believe it to be powerful, *practically* or *functionally*—in the here and now.

There is no relationship in such an irreparable state—that goes beyond the power of Jesus—for it to be restored, reconciled and redeemed—for His glory and by His grace.

Here is the reality friends: You do not get married to the *right* person. You get married to *become* the right person. Marriage is not meant for you to be *happy*—it is meant for you to become *holy*. But when you are pursuing holiness, this is when you will experience the most happiness.

If you love Jesus, you can do whatever you want to do—because what you will want to do—is exactly what Jesus wills for you to do. If you are seeking and loving Jesus with an undivided heart, a cleansed soul, grace fueled strength and a sober mind—God will lead you to your intended spouse and will keep you with your intended spouse.

Being a soul-mate is a two-fold principle. It is both positional and practical:

Positional: A husband and a wife are soul mates in that the two became one flesh. The process of leaving and cleaving has been completed. You are spiritually, emotionally and physically, united to one another.

Practical: The practical aspect of the marriage is being worked out in the day-to-day life of the couple. This beautiful covenant created by God must not just be worked on for the *wedding day*, but also in the *day-to-day*. As a husband seeks to love his wife as Christ loves the church—and as the wife seeks to submit and respect her husband as the Bible teaches—the "soul-mate'ness" of one another intensifies. Couples don't split up because they don't love each other. Couples split up because they don't love Jesus more than they love one another. Instead of being committed to the marriage, both spouses need to commit to the person that they married.

This is the beauty of an intentionally gospel-centered marriage. It is a divine dance that you get better at with age. When both spouses love Jesus more than they love one another—their love for one another will be fueled by one another.

Chapter 8

WHAT WOMEN AND MEN WANT

Husbands, love your wives, as Christ loved
the church and gave himself up for her
(Eph. 5:25)

*"Relationships thrive when we put aside what someone
deserves and respond by giving them what they need."*

I know that I am entering dangerous territory here, but in the spirit of the book, we are going to go ahead and go *forward*. I'm not claiming to be an expert but I have learned a few things along my marriage journey. Here are ten things that women want:

1. **Undivided attention.** She just wants you to pay attention to her. Without you being distracted by anything else. Have a conversation, fully engaged.

2. **Listening, instead of solving.** Sometimes, you just need to listen to what she has to say, instead of trying to solve whatever it is that she has an issue with. The solution part will come in due time. But often, just the act of listening is ninety percent of the solution.

3. **Demonstrate kindness, frequently.** Small acts of kindness that are done often go a long way. It does not have to be something grand, in order for it to make an impact. A sticky note with a short message about how much you love her. Doing a simple chore around the house, without being asked. Keep it simple and frequent.

4. **Plan out date night, ahead of time.** Make all the arrangements, and let her know when and what you will be doing. It's not so much about the surprise but rather about proper planning and making it a great experience.

5. **Notify her of plans, in advance.** Guys think in basic compartments. Here is the box with getting something to eat. Here is another box that has to do with work. Here is another one that deals with leisure. Women think about a lot of things, all the time. And somehow, all those things are connected. So when you plan out your week, let your spouse or significant other know what you are planning. My wife and I always have a sync-up before a week begins so that we both know exactly what we are doing. This eliminates any scheduling conflicts.

6. **Do things, when asked the first time.** Complete the request immediately and faithfully.

7. **Love with more doing, less talking.** Show your spouse or significant other that you love her, with action. Romantic prose needs to be paired with an actualization of what you whisper gently into her ear.

8. **Take responsibility.** If you screwed up, admit it, ask for forgiveness and move on. Don't blame shift. Don't become an expert archeologist by thinking of past mistakes that she made. Do what your great-grandfather Adam did not do.

9. **Make sure she feels safe.** Women are wired to desire protection and security. However you need to display and provide that, go ahead and do it.

10. **Love her like Christ loved the church.** Guys, women are meant to be loved by you, not to be understood by you. So make every effort to love her, in an understanding way.

To my great surprise, I learned that the marriage is not about me. It is about my wife. And the great thing is this: when I make everything about her—the favor is reciprocated in greater measure than in which it was extended! A simple concept but a tough one to actualize during the mundane routine of life. By God's grace, I am attempting to live out Eph. 5:25. I cannot possibly love my wife as much as Christ loved the church. But, I can attempt to do so. I want to please my wife. I want to do what she likes. I want to serve her. I want her to feel loved. I want her to feel special. I want to pleasantly surprise her. This does not come naturally. In fact, some days this does not happen at all. I fail at this when I derail from focusing on what Christ did for me, in my place on the cross. This gospel that I mention so frequently is not something that has happened at one time. It is something that continues to happen in the mean time. This means of grace is the only vehicle by which I can forget about myself and focus on my spouse.

Ladies, here are ten things that men want:

1. **Instructions.** I know you want us to figure out what to do. But please, just give us some basic instructions. We love instructions. We are good with them. If you give me a detailed list of what to do, consider it done.

2. **Encouragement.** When I brush my teeth, tell me that I did a good job. When I go to work, let me know that I am going to crush it today. When I finish a project, let me know how amazing we are together. Encouragement is fuel for guys.

3. **Respect.** This comes in the form of validation. We crave validation. No matter the size of the task or project. Let us know that you are observing what we are doing and that you are proud of our progress.

4. **Coach with compassion.** We have no issue taking some good coaching. But it's not *what* you say, but rather *how* you say it. When coaching, avoid using superlatives. *"You never do this,"* or *"You always get lost,"* does not really help at all. Instead say something like this: *"How can I help you find where we are going,"* or *"What can I do to help you get this accomplished."*

43

5. **Tell us what you want.** I know that you want us to figure out exactly what you want, always. But it's not that easy. Contrary to popular belief, we are not mind readers. At least give some really good hints.

6. **Saying "*I love being your wife.*"** Once you say this, the motivation and dedication to serve you and do everything for you sky-rockets. Try this today. Text him right now.

7. **Saying "*You are appreciated.*"** Guys love hearing this. Again, this is fuel for the road. Say it as often as you can.

8. **Noticing right decisions.** Verbalize the fact that the decision your husband made was a wise one. This again perpetuates his position as a leader and provides motivation for him to continue being that leader.

9. **Specific prayer.** Mention your husband or significant other when you pray together. Specifically say the needs that he has, when you are praying together. This really accentuates the fact that you both are a team—a force to be reckoned with.

10. **Be supportive, but unimpressed.** Don't worship us. Instead support us in what we are doing. This keeps our ego grounded and provides us an honest view of who we really are.

Chapter 9

THE FRIEND ZONE

A friend loves at all times.
(Prov. 17:17a)

"I don't necessarily have to agree with you to be friends with you."

*O*ver the years, I have noticed a common trend with the friendships that I have formed. Every single person that remains my close friend today can tell you that what I am about to share has been present in our interactions.

Forming relationships with other people involves a lot of work. You must be ready to give sacrificially, let your guard down, be let down or be left behind. This is inevitable. This will happen. It is a part of life. However, there are some things that will enable you to form firm friendships that can potentially last a life time.

But before we get there, I want to mention briefly two types of relationships that people usually form:

1. **Cause-Centered:** This first relationship type fuels the fire at first but quickly wanes and falters because it is *cause-centered*. You befriend someone simply because you share an affinity for something. It might be a clothing style, a favorite food, a tech-gadget obsession, a vocation selection, a common school, a ministry project or your passion about particular events. There is nothing wrong with this *per se*. However, many of these things are temporal in nature and fleeting in character. Your sense of style will evolve. You will graduate and eventually go to a different school. You might become an Apple convert and shun all of your Windows friends. The point is that these types of friendships are built upon a sandy foundation that will wash away with the first storm. They are not grounded upon anything that can withstand the test of time.

2. **Cross-Centered:** This type of friendship is based on an affinity that will exist for eternity. You might disagree entirely about food, fanfare and how to have fun. But, you are firmly together when it comes to declaring Jesus as Lord and incarnating gospel principles into your life. Every test that your friendship may go through is looked at through the lens of the gospel. You are not in it because of selfish reasons, affinity or proximity. You both love Jesus and this is the concrete foundation upon which your friendship is built. Your style will evolve, you might switch schools or majors. But, these things do not impact or affect your friendship. The tie that binds you together cannot be

easily broken. It is firmly fixed in place because Jesus is the common unifier in both of your lives.

How can you form firm friendships that are *cross*-centered? What specific elements need to be present in order for your relationships to withstand the test of time and weather the upcoming storms? What separates the *cause* and *cross* centered friendships? How come you are no longer friends with *some* people and absolutely cannot get enough of *other* people? I cannot think of a more practical picture to illustrate the right answer than what I read written in Acts 2:42-47:

And they devoted themselves to the apostles' **teaching** and the **fellowship**, to the **breaking of bread** and the **prayers**. And awe came upon every soul, and many wonders and signs were being done through the apostles. And all who believed were **together** and had all **things in common**. And they were **selling their possessions** and belongings and **distributing the proceeds** to all, as any had need. And day by day, **attending the temple together** and **breaking bread in their homes**, they received their food with glad and generous hearts, praising God and having favor with all the people. And the Lord added to their number day by day those who were being saved.

In this passage, we see how the early church was engaged in fellowship and was able to form firm friendships with one another. I can clearly see from my own personal experience that many of the things mentioned in this text are also visible in my life. This is the only reason why many of my long-standing friendships with people are still vibrant and active even to this day.

Here are five ways you can form firm friendships:

1. **Share a meal,** *together.* This point alone has brought me
   closer to people more so than any sermon I preached, any
   advice I have given or any event I have hosted. Few things
   bring people closer together than sharing a meal together.
   Eating together is proven to deepen your relationship.
   Ask someone out to lunch today and start to form that
   firm friendship over your favorite food. It is a win-win
   situation.

2. **Pray,** *together.* This does not have to be an official prayer
   meeting. Recently, before I sat down to eat, I asked the
   people with whom I was breaking bread with the following
   question: *What prayer needs do you have so that I can pray for*
   you? Just ask this simple question and pray for the other
   person. Pray with someone over the phone if you want.
   When people pray together, they tend to stay together as
   friends, more often than not.

3. **Worship,** *together.* This can happen in any number of
   different venues. Whether it is in your local church, at a
   Christian conference or in a small group bible study. The
   point is that you are doing this, *together.* This past summer,
   I went to a Christian conference with a group of young
   people from my church. The worship experience was epic.
   Singing *In Christ Alone* with the people I pray with, have
   lunch with and worship with, along with other like-minded
   believers—is permanently and pleasantly imprinted in my
   memory.

4. **Sit under the teaching of God's word, *together*.** Something supernatural happens when you sit with people, listening to the preaching of God's word—and you are in the same space, physically. When you are living life during the week, you are on the same diet of Scripture. I love it when during my weekly interactions, people bring up the Sunday sermon and how it has impacted their life. It is akin to a family coming together to hear the dad or mom speak wisdom into their life. That wisdom is then funneled through hearts and fuels the life during the entire week. Firm friendships are silently being formed when we sit together under the reforming Word of God.

5. **Fulfill the needs of one another, *together*.** We live in an age of such sheer abundance that we may think everyone around us has everything they need. This is not entirely the case. A while back, my wife and I decided to dispose of two patio chairs that we were no longer using. We placed them beside the disposal unit in the designated area. A few weeks later, we were returning from an event to our home. As we pull in to park our car, we both glance at our neighbors patio that happens to be on the second floor, overlooking the parking area. To our pleasant surprise, we see our two patio chairs, standing there, being utilized. Apparently, the chairs were not as worn out as we thought. So the next time you are cleaning out your closet or going through your garage—be mindful of the people in your life—and see if you are able to share any of your possessions. Be of service to someone and remain humble enough to be served by others.

In all of the above ways, the common unifier is the concept of doing things *together*. Regardless of whether it is a short lunch, a cup of coffee or setting up chairs for the church service—do this together so that firm friendships can be formed.

You need to center your relationships around Jesus. This is the only foundation upon which your friendships will withstand the test of time.

Chapter 10

FRIENDS, FANS AND TROLLS

If possible, so far as it depends on you, live peaceably with all.
(Rom. 12:18)

"If you don't want to get criticized, don't do anything."

If you don't want to get criticized, don't do anything. But even for that, you will get criticized. There are really only two things that can happen because of criticism. It can either destroy you, or it can refine you. I believe that the best thing to do is to turn your critics into coaches.

Criticism for anyone is normal. It does not matter if what you do is visible. It does not matter if you mostly work in the background. Criticism is inevitable. It will sometimes come from the most surprising of sources. It can sting. It can be painful. It can also be constructive. It can also be productive.

The question is not whether you will experience criticism or not. The better question is this: How do you or how should you react when you receive some sort of criticism. How do you deal with it? What should be your approach? What should be your reaction? How can your attitude towards critics and criticism resemble a Christo-centric mentality?

It is extremely important to distinguish between the different types of critics. This will help you in your growth as a leader and as a person who wisely sifts through counsel directed towards you.

Here are the three types of critics:

1. **Friends.** These people are genuinely interested in your personal growth. They have no personal agenda. They are not practicing partiality towards you. They sincerely see in you great potential and want to maximize your talents. They encourage without being back-slappers. They rebuke without breaking you down. They offer constructive feedback that is palatable and effective. If you are in the wrong, they will call you out on it. But, they will do it in such a way where you will sense the love and will want to change. They approach you with love that issues from a pure heart, a good conscience and a sincere faith (1 Tim. 1:5).

Your Reaction: Spend more time with friends and encourage coaching as often as possible. They are happy to provide it and do so in a productive manner.

2. **Fans.** Fans are people who have neither an affectionate love for you nor do they harbor bitter anger toward you. They know who you are and know what you are all about. They simply see things from a different perspective. Their feedback will not be as restrained as that of the coaches. Some of what they say is great counsel. Counsel which you will not agree with from the beginning. Occasionally, their criticism will be sprinkled with some sort of agenda or activism. They don't really have anything against you. At the same time, they are not too crazy about you either.

Your Reaction: Be cordial and respectful when listening to their counsel. As my seminary professor always said: "Chew the meat and spit out the bones." This should be your method of operation with fans.

3. **Trolls.** This type of critic is the most potent and painful of them all. They are out to either hurt you or use you. They are unreasonable in their demands. They remain unteachable when approached. If you engage in conversation with them, your energy will be depleted and you will leave from their presence degraded. They really do not like who you are or what you are all about. Your presence in their midst literally repels them. They can't quite point out anything legitimately wrong with you. Except the fact that they do not like you. You will most likely never find out the true reason for their dislike of you. At times, they will resort to ungrounded character accusations.

Your Reaction: Sometimes, you have to love people at a distance. Avoid feeding the trolls at all costs. Declare a hunger strike. The Apostle Paul says that if possible, so far as it depends on you, live peaceably with all (Rom. 12:18). Attempt to accept that which they say with sincerity and humility. Avoid getting into arguments or quarrels with this type of critic. If they continue in their vile ways, ignore them and do not let their accusation detract you from your mission.

Whatever type of critic you experience, your approach should be that of a distinctly gospel-infused mentality. Continue to show honor, respect and humility when listening to criticism.

Study what Jesus did when he responded to his critics and follow his example. Make sure you take what He did in the right context. At the same time, use your gift of discernment. Avoid foolish arguments and useless controversies. Ask the Holy Spirit to lead you in handling critics in a Christ-centered manner.

Part Three

CONQUER YOURSELF

"If you want to be a great leader, you must first learn to be a faithful servant."

Chapter 11

MY DREADED CONFESSION

If we confess our sins, he [Jesus] is faithful and just to forgive
us our sins and to cleanse us from all unrighteousness.
(1 Jn. 1:9)

*"There is nothing that can ever be uncovered about you that has
not already been covered for you, by the gospel of Jesus Christ."*

I have a confession to make:

Quitting *anything* and *everything* has crossed my mind,
more than a few times, including writing and finishing this
book.

But here is the reason why even though I have contemplated
it, I never went through with it:

The crazy thing about quitting is that it becomes a viable option to relieve you of fear. Whatever it is that you are facing, is causing you to experience anxiety or frustration. So, the natural inclination for us humans is to simply press the eject button. To shut it down. To throw in the towel. To stick a fork in it and consider it done. You get the picture.

Even though this might be the easiest option, it most certainly is not the best option, neither is it the wisest. Here are the top four things that people usually quit for ridiculous reasons:

1. **Jobs.** A lot of people think that they can do a half-way job at their day job and miraculously score their dream job. But if you can't do your day job faithfully, what makes you think you can do your dream job, excellently? Some of us don't need better work, we just need to do the work we have, better. I have worked in super micro-managed environments, where my every move was monitored and tracked. I have worked in environments where I have freedom in creating my own schedule. Here is the thing: At the end of the day, both require work and effort. If you quit your current job, the next job will still have the same thing you have to do. It is called *work*. That doesn't change. You can change the external scenery, but that won't make up for your lack of diligence in doing a job you were assigned to do.

2. **Relationships.** A lot of people quit relationships, consistently. They are like serial quitters. Why? Because someone did not fulfill my desire, my request or my need. So people often go from one relationship, to another and again to another. The problem with this serial quitter

business is that eventually, you will have to learn to get along with people. No one is perfect, including you and I. So, you can run from your spouse, your significant other, your friend, your boss or your parents. But the one person you won't be able to run away from, is yourself. If you don't learn how to be effective at building relationships, you will drift from one relationship to another, leaving collateral damage, that someone else will have to pick up. Quitting a relationship won't actually create a better you.

3. **Churches.** The church is a hospital for the broken, not a museum for the beautiful. The great tragedy occurs when we start *going* to church and stop *being* the church. Jesus came to earth and said that the sick are in need of a physician. Often people tell me that they don't want to go to church because it is full of hypocrites. To which I say, *"great, you will fit right in."* A Christian who sins is not a hypocrite but rather human. Whether your church barely has 100 people on any given Sunday, or you have fifty campuses and over fifty thousand people attending, every week, issues will still exist. If you quit a church because your needs were not being met, most likely the problem was in you, not in the church. Some of us don't need a better *church*, we just need to be the church *better.*

4. **Dreams.** Dreams cost time, not money. The reason you are not achieving your dreams is not because you lack resources, or money or support. It is because you are too afraid to face the hard work that lies before you. You let other people define your life for you, instead of trusting the One who created a life, in you. Far too often, we are

like those kids playing with mud pies, while our parents are offering us a vacation on the sea, aboard a luxury yacht.

Don't quit your dream, just because your friends did not make it.
Don't quit your dream, just because it scares you.
Don't quit your dream, just because your peers ridiculed it and declared it impossible.
Don't quit your dream, because it takes too much work.

Anything worth doing, is worth doing well. And before you will get super good at it, you will have to put in some serious effort.

When Jesus saved us, He did so when there was nothing in us, to save us. While we were vile and filthy sinners, Jesus came to earth to die on the cross. Jesus lost His life, so that we have a life.

Jesus did not quit half-way.

He did not quit while He was 12 years old teaching people three times His age.
He did not quit when He was constantly being pursued by people who wanted to kill Him.
He did not quit when His closest disciples had no idea why He kept talking about His impending death.
He did not quit even when He was abandoned by His closest friends.
He did not quit when He was murdered by His fiercest enemies.
He continued on His mission until the very end. He loved us, to die for us.

So before you decide to confess and quit, I want you to consider these five things:

1. **Jesus knows exactly what you are going through.** There is never a single moment when the God of the universe does not care about your situation. He knows exactly what is going on in your life right now. The Scripture admonishes us to call out to Him. He is our source of hope and calm amidst the storms of life. Paul tells the Philippians (Php. 4:6): Do not be anxious. Whatever it is that remains the source of your frustration or hurt— let God know about it. His peace that surpasses even our most discerning understanding—will guard our heart, will calm our heart. The peace of God will envelop us. Never stop believing this. Cry out to God. He *will* hear you. He *does* hear you. He cares *for* you and cares *about* you. Your situation does not determine your position with God. You are continuously His child and He loves you.

2. **Character formation is difficult but valuable.** Jesus said that one who is faithful in a very little is also faithful in much (Lk. 16:19). Maybe you want to quit your job. Maybe you want to quit your marriage. Maybe you want to quit loving people because they are impossible to love. You want to quit the sanctifying process in your life. You want to quit working on a certain relationship. You want to quit putting grace-empowered energy into loving others. I want to encourage you today. Do not quit and do not give up. This is a process that God is putting you through so that you would look more like His Son Jesus, with every single day.

3. **Look at obstacles in your life as opportunities for growth.** If God got you *in* it, God will get you *through* it. You might want to get a higher paying job. You might be craving a more modern worship experience. You might already be done with trying to reach out to a person that is not reciprocating the love. Do not stop. Do not quit. Thrive and excel in the environment that God has put you in right now. Work as unto the Lord. Yes your boss is a Jewish Carpenter! God has given us every single divine blessing that we need in order to be incarnate Christ's in our communities. We lack clarity of God's presence in our life. That is the issue. But that does not mean He is not there, gentle like the wind, slowly forming and shaping us—so that we have the mind of Christ and the thoughts of Christ.

4. **The gospel of Jesus is just as potent and powerful as it always was.** The power of God and the efficiency of Christ's work on the cross is not nullified because of your current situation. God is just as powerful and the Holy Spirit is just as active in your life. If you are feeling like that is not the case, then it is due time to cry out to God in repentance and seek restoration. There is no situation too complex that has not already found its solution at the foot of Jesus' cross. This is a truth that we must believe and preach to ourselves personally, every single day.

5. **Show compassion to the people in your life who are going through a tough time.** Sometimes, people are not looking for a solution to their problem but rather a person that will listen to their problem. All of us are fighting a

battle of some sort. Even when we are in Christ and He is in us. This fallen world does not make it easy. But we are not without hope. As fellow Christians, we must come alongside of those who are hurting, helping them by the power of the Holy Spirit. Maybe this means listening more and speaking less. Maybe this means not saying anything at all but just sitting and spending time with a hurting person. Maybe this means not pulling out Jesus-Jukes every single moment. This practically means looking at people through the lens that God uses to look at us. God looks at us not as we *are* but as Christ *is*. Compassion is not something you say, but something you show. Jesus constantly was filled with compassion and decidedly demonstrated this compassion to other people (Mk. 1:41; Mk. 6:34; Matt. 9:36 Matt. 20:34). We must do the same because we are striving to be like Jesus.

God is *with* us. God is with *us*. Jesus is alive and loves you. Jesus cares for you and will continue to take care of you. You will make it, because Jesus did.

Chapter 12

FAILURE IS NOT FATAL

There is therefore now no condemnation
for those who are in Christ Jesus.
(Rom. 8:1)

*"The most painful part of your biography will become
the most powerful part of your testimony."*

*F*ailure is a part of your life, but it does not have to define your life. Failure should refine, not define us. What matters is not how you failed but what you do following the failure. We have two options when our actions lead to less than pleasurable consequences: We can dwell on it or we can move forward from it. The former will add more anxiety. The latter will allow you to live through it and become better from it.

All of us have made mistakes that could have been avoided. Here is a small sample of examples:

Not following the speed limit
Making a foolish financial decision
Making a damaging decision in an organization
Creating a negative atmosphere based on improper action taken
Saying something that otherwise would have been better left unsaid
Basing your reaction on raging emotions rather than tranquil contemplation
Stifling maturity by focusing the situation on *"you"* and not seeing the bigger picture

No one can flee the fluid flavor of failure. No matter how smart we think we are, failure is inescapable. It is a part of life but should not characterize our life. Some of the most valorous leaders we know have experienced failure:

Moses failed by directly disobeying God thereby eliminating his ability to lead the people into the Promised Land (Nm. 20:12).

Abraham failed by demonstrating unbelief concerning his fertility thereby having an illegitimate son with his maidservant (Gen. 16:1-16).

David failed by performing infidelity with Bathsheba thereby bringing upon himself a calamitous curse of a new-born son's death (2 Sam. 11:12)

Solomon failed by being engaged in licentious and sacrilegious activity with his numerous and flirtatious, femme fatales (1 Kings 11).

Peter failed by denying the Lord Jesus three times immediately following his courageous confession of the exact opposite (Jn. 18:15-18).

Paul failed by being so zealous about persecuting the church, he (initially) entirely missed the Creator of the church (Php. 3:5-7).

How could these people fail? Are not some of them included in the hall of faith (Heb. 11)? Are they not those who are considered to be perpetual pursuers of God's own heart? Are they not instruments God used to bring 3000 & 5000 to repentance and faith in Jesus? Are they not authors who penned the majority of the epistles in the New Testament? Are they not considered the wisest and wealthiest of all the men who walked the earth?

There is a common thread that we see with the above people. They possessed a nature just like ours. They failed and fell down. But, their failure did not determine their future. Even with the enormity of their failure, we are still to imitate and follow them. The deep mercy of God is visible in the deep failure of man.

Failure, although painful is not final. Realizing that you failed is important. What is more important is being intentional about learning a lesson and moving forward. This is what the above people did. This is also what we should do.

Here are seven critical components that have to do with learning from your failure and not letting it define you:

1. **Realize.** We must accept responsibility for our actions. We must first realize that we have failed. We did something we should not have done. We said something we should not have said. We engaged in behavior that should have never characterized us. We have sinned against God and against man. We need to understand it, learn from it and move forward away from it.

2. **Repent.** A sincere acknowledgement of the failure must take place. Regret is not a supplement for repentance. The Bible teaches us to confess our sins to one another (Prov. 28:13; Js. 5:16; 1 Jn. 1:6-9). Our repentance must be clearly verbalized, both publicly and privately. Authenticity and clarity are key components that should accompany your repentance. When repenting, avoid using vague or abstract language. Statements such as "*I am sorry,*" "*I was wrong,*" and "*I committed a sin*" are not popular in our culture today. But, if we want our repentance to include potency, items need to be labeled respectively. Avoid using mild terminology while overlooking the reality. Most people can tell if the repentance is forced and faked or factual and faithful. By repenting, you are acknowledging your depravity *and* your intentionality to change.

3. **Restore.** It is imperative that immediately following a failure, we must seek to restore that which was ruined. Expedience is of the essence. There is no reason to maintain a moratorium on restoration. This should not be

approached with complacency but rather urgency. What specifically is in need of restoration? Every situation is unique. For some it is trust that needs to be earned once more. For others, it might be a financial burden that needs to be repaid. Still for many, it might mean time, energy and resources need to be reestablished for the restorative process to take place.

4. **Reconcile.** This is the component that brings two opposing parties together in an amicable union (Matt. 18:15-19). Nothing else can bring more pleasure to the anxious soul than this. An apology has been extended to the offended party by the offending party. A failure is followed up by a fervent desire to reconcile. The desire for reconciliation should be the motivating force behind every failure. The focus should be taken off of "you" and realigned onto the needs of others. If we love Jesus authentically, this desire should come to us naturally. Regardless of the depth of your failure, reconciliation should be relentlessly pursued. Regardless of the complexity of your situation, reconciliation should be actively attempted.

5. **Reflect.** Recovering from a failure can be a lengthy, painful progression. But, it does not have to be a wasteful process. Use what you have learned to avoid having failure characterize your life in the future. This is most effective when you are reflective of the past. Asking these penetrative questions can help avoid future pitfalls:

Where did I go wrong?
What could I have done differently?

How can I use what I learned to alter my future choices?
What critical component from the above list has not yet been fulfilled?
What specifically do I have a disposition towards that I need to be aware of?
What has this failure taught me about my sinful nature and about my sinless Savior?

6. **Renew.** After a difficult failure in your life, it is important to renew your battered soul. No, I am not talking about secular therapy or self-help books. What I am talking about is intentionally disengaging from the throes of life, temporarily. This might look very different for everyone. Your schedule might or might not allow it. With the proper planning, you are able to do this. The quantity of time is not as is important as the quality of time. It might mean taking a break from some sort of activity that you were always engaged in. Take a Sabbath from something to get a fresh perspective. Disconnect and perform a digital detox. Do your daily devotional in an unfamiliar place. Get out of your comfort zone and your usual social circle. Interact with people who you have never met. Rejuvenation is just as important for you as for the people you have been chosen to lead. You will come back refreshed; they will be ready to receive counsel from a weathered veteran.

7. **Remain.** Now that we have learned this much from failure, we are not going to let it define us. In order for this to be perpetually present in our life, we must be intentional. We must remain in close proximity with Jesus through our spiritual disciplines. We must remain humble and teachable.

We must remain attuned to the Spirit of God speaking into our lives. We must be attuned to the voice of our friends, critics and foes. We must always have a singular focus of glorifying God in our life. This is the single most effective preventative methodology that we can embrace. I am not saying we will never again fail in our life. I am saying that our reaction to future failure will be more holistic in approach. Remain open to criticism and rebuke. Remain cognizant of your depravity. Remain maintaining clarity about the brevity of life. Remain in the presence of Jesus. Remain in His Word. Remain in the company of His people.

Failure, although painful, does not determine your future. Learn from failure and move forward, away from it.

Chapter 13

PAINFUL LESSONS

Let not your hearts be troubled. Believe
in God; believe also in me.
(Jn. 14:1)

*"If you live for the approval of people, you
will die by the rejection from people."*

I preached my first sermon when I was twelve years old. At
that time, I had no idea what God was going to do with
my life. I began to lead my first community group when I was
seventeen. As I traveled through my teens, into my twenties,
the call from God upon my life, intensified. I actually never
dreamed of being a pastor or a leader. Some people are born
with a pulpit built for them. Others are given the pulpit because
before they wanted it, God prepared it for them.

Whenever people ask me if they should go into ministry, I always ask them one simple question:

Do you love people? If you answer *no*, then ministry might not be for you. I have had people literally tell me—*ministry would actually be really awesome, if it were not for the people.*

Jesus ultimately laid His life down for people—those who loved him and those who crucified Him. Ministry is full of amazing and provides a dose of affliction.

Here are ten painful leadership lessons I learned, from ten years of ministry:

1. **Don't be so busy doing the *work* of the Lord, that you entirely neglect the *Lord* of the work.** Ministry is all about Jesus. It is not about how you look. It is about how God looks. It is not about how you are *performing*. It is about how Jesus is *projected*. By you. Faithfulness is more important than excellence. Consistency is more important than frequency. Do the work. Do your best. Get some rest. Simple.

2. **Don't be crushed by criticism.** You will have critics. The question is not *if* you will get criticized. The question is *when* you will get criticized. I bet it will be pretty soon. Some critics are harsh. Some are gentle. Some constructive. Some destructive. Chew the meat, and spit out the bones. Turn your critics into coaches. Your critics do not determine your future, Jesus does. If you live for the approval of people, then you will die from the rejection of people.

3. **Don't be puffed up by compliments.** Treat a compliment as you would a criticism. Remain indifferent towards it. Be courteous. Be grateful. Give glory to Jesus. Keep moving forward.

4. **Don't bask in your own glory.** Big heads are often connected to small hearts. Encouragement is awesome. Receive it. But know this: Confidence will get you started, but persistence will keep you going. Persistence keeps working, long after the compliments are gone.

5. **Friends will masquerade as fans.** You will meet people who like what you are about *generally*, but do not like you, *personally*. They are all about your vision, but want nothing to do with the one casting the vision. They love projects, but don't want to put in time during the process. If Jesus had a tough time, so will we. We worship Someone who was abandoned by his closest friends—and murdered by the fiercest of fans. No one said the life of a disciple would be easy.

6. **Empower people.** Micromanaging is dead. Excel at what you are good at and let others excel at what they are good at. Allow people to stumble and fall. They learn quicker that way. Be there to help them up. Be tough and tender. We are all on the same team, wearing the same jersey, rooting for the same Jesus.

7. **Ardent supporters become agenda activators.** Beware when being consistently complimented. Jesus said: "woe to you, when all people speak well of you" (Luke 6:26).

8. **Do not believe your own press.** You are not that good. Sometimes, the most vocal of supporters, become the most unpleasant individuals. Follow the wise words of James and do not practice partiality (James 2:1-9).

9. **Your words carry more weight.** It is not *what* you say, but *how* you say it. What is said is important. But *who* said it, is even more important. Choose your words carefully. Better to be thought a fool, than to open your mouth and prove it.

10. **Your every action will be under careful inspection.** If someone does not like you, they will try to dig stuff up to support their perilous plan. Your Facebook posts will be sifted through. Your conversations will be recorded. Not as fun as it sounds. Take heed to what Paul says to a young pastor: Watch your life and doctrine closely. Do not practice what you preach. Preach what you practice. Without spot or blemish. A shepherd should be above reproach. In every sphere.

A true leader is one who is constantly aware of the needs of other people and serves them to the best of their ability for the glory of Jesus and the joy of those whom he is serving. Jesus reiterated this point when he washed the feet of the disciples, a task reserved for the lowliest of servants. He said to his disciples that the one who is greater is the one who serves (Luke 22:27).

Chapter 14

WILL THE REAL MEN PLEASE STAND

Do nothing from selfish ambition or conceit, but in
humility count others more significant than yourselves.
(Php. 2:3)

*"Real manhood is about displaying the Great
Hero, instead of trying to be the hero."*

Will the real men please stand up? This is a crisis call to our generation today. We have a catastrophe of epic proportions where real men are few and far between. These are issues that are constantly in my mind as I wrestle with the hope of what I want to be, and the reality of what I am, currently. I fail often, but the great thing is that Jesus extends His grace, continuously. If you are not being led by Jesus well, you will have a tough time leading others well.

Society, culture and mass media have absolutely destroyed what a real man looks like. Men today are portrayed as lazy, inattentive buffoons who can't accomplish much, only want sex from their spouse or significant other, desire to consume alcohol continuously and at least hold a job where they can provide the minimal necessities for their family. Think of the popular cartoon *The Simpsons*. At least there, a nuclear family is displayed where the husband and wife have never been divorced and the two spouses are a different gender. That is already very shocking to the culture that we live in. But still, the husband (*Homer*) is known as they guy who skips work to go to the local bar. He is not really good at his job and regularly is in trouble with his boss. He is not very intelligent and is always being one-upped by either his wife or daughter regarding basic life knowledge.

To say that we have a crisis of manhood in our society today, would be an understatement. Our culture has a very warped view of what a real man looks like. Usually, movies portray a real man who beats up on other bad guys, who is a womanizer, moving from one female interaction to the next, can swing a hammer and does not dress like a european metrosexual. Is that really what a real man looks like? Even if we put the twisted Hollywood culture aside, how about the cultural idea of what a man really is? He needs to dress a certain way, doesn't wear skinny jeans, usually does not care much about his hygiene and spends his free time at Lowe's and Home Depot.

He is the man who has the final say in every decision made in the home, will pound his fist on the kitchen table if his authority is questioned and usually needs some industrial soap to clean his hands after a long day of working with his hands. Is that the definition of Biblical manhood? That a man needs to be rough, rugged and tough? That he needs to be able to fix anything or remodel an entire home in one weekend? Depending on your cultural upbringing, you will answer with a resounding amen or not, to this question. While there is a hint of truth to all of the above descriptions of men, and most men do have those qualities—I don't think that is the proper definition of what a real man is made of.

I don't care how culture or media or Hollywood pitches to me what a real man looks like. I care about what the Bible says and how God defines what a real man looks like and what a real man does. Here is my short definition of what a real man, made in the image of God, looks like and does:

Real manhood is not about being macho, harsh or domineering. It's about possessing a quiet strength that has been surrendered to God, displaying the great Hero, instead of trying to be the hero.

God created the man to be the leader, the protector and the cultivator. Notice that God did not create a man to be a harsh dictator, the dominator or an abuser of women. Here are seven traits that I believe a real man, made in the image of God, has and displays consistently:

1. **He demonstrates a quiet strength.** The man who emulates Jesus is strong but gentle. He is tough, but tender. He is able to exercise authority, without having to verbalize

that he is the authority. Once you have to actually tell people that you have authority, you have already lost it.

2. **He is fatherly, but not necessarily a father to anyone biologically.** A man can display a fatherly love to others, without having any biological children of his own. To demonstrate the attentiveness and compassion of a father, you are not required to have children of your own. Some of the greatest men that have ever lived, displaying the love and strength of a father, did not actually have any children.

Jesus never had any children, yet He instructs us to cry out to Him as *Abba*, or *daddy*.

The Apostle Paul, who had no children, says that He was dealing with the Thessalonians as a father, deals with his own children—encouraging, comforting, and urging them to live lives worthy of God (1 Thess. 2:11).

The great german theologian Dietrich Bonhoeffer did not have any biological children.

Pope John Paul II did not have any children.

George Washington, who is named as the father of our country, also did not have any biological children.

3. **He displays integrity in all that he does.** He pursues a lifestyle of moral excellence, being molded and shaped by Jesus. He says what he means, and means what he says. There is no difference between his public and private life.

4. **He has a Christ-like character.** We need more character, and less characters. The real measure of a man's character is what he would do if no one found out. The real man thinks about fanning into flame his relationship with Jesus, and how he can practically be Jesus to his wife, his family, his community, his church and every sphere of life that he finds himself in.

5. **He is humble and teachable.** Humility is super shy. As soon as you start talking about it, it runs away. This is why this trait is a bit tough to actually point out. Humility is repenting and asking forgiveness first. Humility is thinking of yourself less. Humility is expediently admitting that you were wrong, and apologizing. Humility is putting your machismo and bravado aside, and admitting that you are weak and incapable, without Jesus.

6. **He does not quit on his wife, his family or his church.** A real man does not walk out on his family. A real man does not bow down to becoming a coward, because life gets tough or there is no light at the end of the tunnel. He does not quit when the going gets tough. A real man does not have a wandering eye or a mind full of fantasy, where his wife is conspicuously absent. A real man, provides for his family, just like Jesus provides for us. A real man lays down his life for the people closest to him, just like Jesus laid down His life for every single one of us. A real man loves his wife passionately, loves his family deeply and loves his church greatly.

7. **He consistently presses into and imitates the greatest man who every lived, Jesus Christ.** A real man looks

to Jesus and becomes the practical savior to the people in his life. He chooses to do the *right* thing, instead of the *sure* thing. His first priority is the well-being of his wife, his family or the people around him. He is fueled by the desire to be like Jesus, instead of the desire to be acclaimed or recognized.

We would have a cultural revolution and a radical strengthening of families in our world, if the above seven traits were espoused by all men, whether single or married. Only by looking to Jesus, the greatest Man that ever lived, can we as men come even close to being exactly what we were created to be.

Chapter 15

RADICAL COMMITMENT TO THE ORDINARY

One who is faithful in a very little is also faithful in much
(Luke 16:10a)

"God loves to do the incredible through the ordinary."

*B*eing *radical* is the latest craze these days. Sell your house. Sell your car. Sell your possessions. Step out in faith. Don't worry about anything. God will provide. If it is God's will, it is God's bill. But if everyone sells their house, quits their job and sells all of their possessions—how will all those people who acted so radically be supported? Who will fund the plane ticket to Haiti? Who will provide financial support to build that fresh water well? What if you have nothing to sell and no possessions to pawn?

We do not hear of the faithful Christian who works forty hours a week, provides for his family and still has money left over to fund these projects. There is no slick video flick that accentuates the daily traffic jam they endure. There are no social media masses gathering to see how they have a Bible study with their kids. Yet because of this *mundane* life style, a *radical* life style can be perpetuated for some.

I meet young people all the time who want to turn the world upside down for Jesus. I love hearing your enthusiasm. I love hearing your passion. I love hearing your desire to step out in faith, call a local grocer, and have them feed for free—twenty thousand people who gathered in a humanitarian clinic—in an inner city neighborhood.

But there is a disconnect between the radical and the reality. Someone needed to put in some hours to make the miracle available. Most people who can afford to do the radical— are people who have an abundant amount of resources—in finances and connections. So this is the irony behind trying to live radically. If every Christian began to live radically—then there would be no Christian mechanics, baristas, customer service agents, nurses, doctors, attorneys, gardeners and fill in the blank. Who will then provide the financial support for these rugged and rogue radicals, building orphanages and siphoning clean drinking water out of polluted springs?

I am full speed ahead with being radical. But living *radically* must be married to a thing called *responsibility*. Call me crazy (or *radical*), but here are three ways that you and I can become rogue radicals, without leaving the country, without quitting our job and without trying to irresponsibly put God to the test:

1. **Read Your Bible Every Single Day.** Super radical, I know. Can you imagine if everyone you knew, actually read their Bible every single day? It does not sound as exciting as traveling to a foreign country—to take pictures with a phone that probably cost you more than an entire annual wage of the most wealthiest person present. Imagine the radical change you would see in your life and the lives of people around you.

2. **Believe In The Gospel.** Jesus is just as radically alive in a hipster coffee shop in Seattle, in a fog-enveloped fish and chips joint in San Francisco or at a distressed slum in Sao Paulo. Believe that the gospel is real when you get a flat tire. Believe that the gospel is real when you lose your job. Believe that the gospel is radical when someone else gets that promotion you were eyeing for half a decade. Believe that the gospel is just as powerful and radical in your every day life—as it is displayed in a foreign country.

3. **Embrace Your Current Life Narrative.** I have a radically explosive idea: How about going all out and radically committing to serving in a local church? How about a radical abandonment of always praising your podcast pastor and giving some props to your local pastor. How about dangerously surrendering your time spent watching your favorite sitcom and actually serving your community—in a tangible way. How about being a reckless/radical rebel by adhering to punctually attending a community group,

a church service, your job or the meeting you nonchalantly cancel via a text message.

Jesus calls us to follow Him with reckless abandonment. We must be radically deliberate to display a gospel-centered faithfulness—in the mundane and trivial parts of our life.

We are not being radical when we seek some exotic mission to fulfill our calling as disciples of Jesus. We are not being radical when we hyper-spiritualize everything, when we devalue the local over the global or when we seek the thrill instead of being content with the chill.

We are being rogue radicals when we embrace the ordinary, the mundane and the seemingly un-exciting aspects of our life—and realize that Jesus is still powerful and potent—even without stage lights or jeep rides through the safari.

God loves to do the incredible through the ordinary, the unbelievable through the faithful, the exciting through the mundane everyday. If we are not intentionally present, we might miss God's presence. We are so busy chasing the miraculous, we end up missing the divine during the mundane.

You have one life to live you ordinary *radical*—make it count. Go. *Forward*.

Part Four

CREATE AMAZING

"Dreams without deadlines are mere fantasies."

Chapter 16

CLEAR THE CLUTTER

Therefore, since we are surrounded by so great a
cloud of witnesses, let us also lay aside every weight,
and sin which clings so closely, and let us run
with endurance the race that is set before us
(Heb 12:1)

"Your circumstances are not holding you back, your attitude is."

I cannot work in an environment that is messy or
unorganized. When I sit down in my office, I make sure
that the table at which I am sitting is free from any debris and
distraction. When my work space is cleaner, I breathe easier. If
I have a pile of paperwork on my desk, I usually go through it,
arrange it, shred what I don't need and continue on with the
task I was about to start. If my office is unorganized, so too

will be my thinking process when I begin to write something. The first thing I do is clear the clutter.

The primary reason why we don't have clarity in our life is because we have not cleared out the clutter from our life. I define clarity as the rigorous ability to definitively know *what* you are doing, what you *want* to do, *where* you are now and *how* you are going to get where you want to be. Clarity is achieved when you have a crystal clear realization of your God given abilities and how you will use them to bring God maximum glory and spread contagious joy to the people around you.

Gaining and maintaining maximum clarity is a concept that was rigorously practiced by Jesus. Jesus achieved and maintained maximum clarity in His life. During his whole tenure here on earth, He was absolutely obsessed with one thing: **Fulfilling the will of His Father** (Jn. 4:34; 5:30; 6:38-39; Matt. 12:50). This is all that he cared about and exclusively what he focused on.

He preached the gospel because this was the will of His Father. He discipled and trained men because this would fulfill the will of His Father. He knew this would ultimately fuel the explosion of the gospel message for the salvation of those who believed. He did not attempt to open up a supernatural hardware store. He did not do miracles just so that he would amass more followers.

Jesus was discriminative in *what* he did, *when* he did it, *how* he did it and *why* He did it. From a profoundly young age (Lk. 2:49) and long before beginning his public ministry, Jesus had a crystal clear understanding of his mission:

To live a life we could not live, to die a death we could not die and to bear the sin we could not atone for.

If we want to lead a life that is well lived, we need to understand this concept of clarity and begin to apply it actively. By doing this, we are able to make a bigger impact for the gospel, leave a legacy that will make a permanent imprint on other people and fulfill our God given role during our God given time on this God created earth.

Here are nine things you can do right now to clear the clutter and gain maximum clarity in your life:

1. **Pray specifically.** From my own personal experience, specificity in prayer is absolutely necessary. Before I even met my wife, I prayed like crazy about my future wife for about five years. I prayed that God would send into my life a godly woman who could be my wife. I prayed that my marriage would be a reflection of what Jesus is all about. My *prayer* life facilitated the clarity to be existent *in* my life. The Bible teaches us that when we lack wisdom, we should pray for it (Js. 1:5). It will then be given to us, with no questions asked. This is the first thing you should do right now.

2. **Pray strategically.** Stop and pray. Pray and ask God for the following: God, what specifically would you like me to do in my life—in a way that would bring you maximum glory. God, what area in my life do I need to reassess in order to radically re-align it with your will for my life. God, where in my life have I lost focus? God, please ensure

that my life is centered on your Son Jesus Christ. God, please work *in* me so that you could do a great work *through* me. God, please allow me to understand for how long of a season you have put me in this particular job. God, please make me as impactful as possible, in the area of influence that you have given me. God, relieve me of my obsession with my personal preferences and allow me to specifically align myself with your will for my life.

3. **Learn to say NO.** You have to learn to say no to *good* things so that you can say yes to *great* things. When your plate is full and is about to break, you are of no help to anyone and have become a hazard to yourself. The crazy part is that sometimes, you will have to learn to say no to things that you absolutely love doing. I am notorious for not saying no to certain requests. A few months ago, I planned out a weekend trip. In this trip, I was out of state for two days. During that trip, I hosted a party and spoke three different times during a two day time period. I flew back home feeling like I got hit by a truck. I wish I would have applied this principle. I would have been more beneficial to the people I was serving. My energy level and my clarity of thought would have been clearer had I not overbooked myself.

4. **Be assertive when saying NO.** This will be extremely difficult for you to do when you do it for the first time. People might not understand how you could say no when they always remember you being a yes-man (woman). In order to have clarity in your life, you will have to learn to say no to things in your life. God has given you time to use

and you are demanded to be a wise steward of it. Should not every request you get be filtered through with this specific mindset?

5. **Assess before agreeing.** Remember, you do not have to do *everything* and you do not have to answer a resounding yes to *every* single request. Before agreeing to something, always let the person know that you need some time to think about it. Then, assess the request in light of the clarity commitment you have for your life. Ask yourself the following questions: Will this be the best use of my time? Is this task propelling me to a deeper level of clarity in my life? Am I the best fit for this task or position? Is there someone else who can benefit from doing this and my skills as a coach could be shown and sharpened?

6. **Maintain exclusivity in your focus.** When I was growing up, I wanted to be a lot of things. I wanted to do a lot of things. After watching The Boiler Room one evening, I wanted to become a stock broker. After working for a car rental lot, I wanted to own my own car rental company. After working in a retail game store, I wanted to create board games for a living. After working in a windshield replacement clinic, I thought I was going to make a fortune searching for dime-sized cracks from unfortunate motorists. After working at a market research company, I thought I was going to form and host focus groups surrounding new products being introduced to the market. My mind was racing a million miles a minute in a million different directions. Everything excited me. Everything still does. The difference between now and then is that now, I have

a crystal clear understanding about where my talents and abilities are and how I can use them to bring maximum glory to God and contagious joy to the people in my life.

7. **Crave constructive feedback.** I realized that I was not fit to turns shacks into chateaus, like my father was able to. After writing hundreds of essays in high school, college and graduate school, I realized that few things in life bring me more pleasure and joy than writing. I also realized that I can form at least a few sentences together and say something useful for others to hear. That last part can of course be debated. I am still in the process of learning. If you want to achieve a maniacal level of clarity, you must become exclusive in your focus. This won't happen overnight, but it will happen over time. You just have to be extremely intentional about uncovering what your focus should be. Here is how to do this: Ask your spouse, your family, your friends and your co-workers. Remain humble to receive constructive feedback. They have a better perspective and are well positioned to tell you what you should focus on. They can tell you where your abilities are most apparently visible.

8. **Remove the clutter.** Clean your room. Clean your office. Arrange, organize and situate everything in a way that will make the environment conducive for maximum output. Thankfully, my wife helped me recently to rearrange my office. We removed all the clutter and created a simple environment with minimal distraction. The same way that we must do this with our physical work space, we must also do with the space in our mind. What is cluttering your

mind right now? Is there something you need to repent of of? Is there a reconciliation that needs to occur? The Bible teaches us to *lay aside lay aside every weight, and sin which clings so closely, and let us run with endurance the race that is set before us* (Heb. 12:1). Before you can remove the clutter from your life, you must clearly identify that which clings to your life, disallowing you to achieve maximum clarity.

9. **Maintain narrow focus.** What one thing in your life right now is preventing you from achieving maximum clarity? What is that one thing? Remove it. Get rid of it. Clean it up. Dispose of it. If you want to gain clarity in your life, you must remove the clutter from your life. Start with something small like cleaning your office or work area. Delete the apps off of your phone that you never use. Clean out your wallet, purse or man-bag. Remove yourself from activities that are burning you out. Avoid over committing to events that you physically do not have time for. You are going to feel a sense of relief after you do this.

Chapter 17

SLAY YOUR DRAGONS

So, whether you eat or drink, or whatever
you do, do all to the glory of God.
(1 Cor. 10:31)

*"If you want to make a difference in the world, you need
to learn to wake up before the rest of the world."*

In the early morning, before the sun has risen—they are lurking and plotting. Mercy is not their forte and sympathy is not on their agenda. They creep up on you in the most unassuming of ways. You can see the enticing glow, but just know that it is a trap. Blinking and buzzing, notifying and distracting. Hiding your essentials and camouflaging your tools. You stumble around in what seems like a familiar environment—but for some reason—you cannot find anything that you are looking for.

These creatures are strategic in their approach and unwavering in their intent: To amuse, throw off and disorient—before the dawn has yet to break. No matter how hard you try to escape their presence—they are still there—ready to do *the* work—so that you won't be able to get *to* work.

I knew that I had to come up with a plan. To slay the dragons and to take back what belongs to me. I knew that if this battle was not won before breakfast—I would face an inevitable defeat. There might still be a slim chance of victory—but highly unlikely. Then it dawned on me. I knew exactly what I had to do.

Here is my seven step defense system that attacks each specific dragon, and slays it—before breakfast:

1. **The Resistance Dragon:** You know you need to prepare for tomorrow. But long before the morning comes—this dragon is already starting to rear its ugly head. Every time you begin to do something productive—your mind drifts effortlessly to some trivial task—that screams for your urgent attention. Destroy this resistance dragon immediately. The greatest demonstration of power is a display of self-control. My counter-attack would begin the night before. I front-load everything. It was calm and quiet. I made time to plan and prepare. After all, the more I strategized in the evening—the closer victory was to me in the morning.

2. **The Food Dragon:** Prepare the fuel the night before. Our bodies are uniquely created machines. They need fuel to keep going, at an effective rate. Prepare what you will eat

and drink for breakfast, *the night before*. Buy the ingredients. Organize them in your fridge. Grind your coffee the night before. Wash your coffee cup and put it on your kitchen counter. Pack your lunch and place the bag in the fridge. When you wake up—this dragon has been already defeated. Grab your nutrients, your coffee and your lunch—success.

3. **The Clothing Dragon.** Think about what you need to wear the night before. No matter if you are fashion conscious or think that Ainsley Collar and Forward Point are cities in the state of Maryland—you still get dressed in the morning. Pick out your outfit. Iron it. Dry clean it. Lay it out. Hang it up. Call it a night. In the morning—you will be glad you did.

4. **The Technology Dragon.** Charge all of your devices, the night before. Put them on *"do not disturb,"* or *"sleep"* mode. Organize your power cords. Put all of your peripherals in your work bag. That way, there are less chances you might have missed something in your morning rush.

5. **The Vehicle Dragon.** Put gas in your tank, the night before. Make sure the car is good to go, before you need to go. In the morning, you will be glad you did.

6. **The Notification Dragon.** This one is the toughest to battle. Go all out in the fight with this one. If you do not defeat this dragon, every other dragon will become much more difficult to conquer. Create a specific time when you will check all of your notifications. Limit yourself to checking them during that one time. Do not multi-task.

7. The False-Estimate Dragon. Create an intentional buffer zone for your entire schedule. Add a buffer zone to your entire commute. Add a buffer zone to all of your meetings. Add a buffer zone for any unexpected or extenuating circumstances. Put the ego on the shelf. You won't make it somewhere in thirty minutes, when it usually takes you one hour. It just won't happen. Or you will have to deal with other dragons, which work well with the false-estimate dragon. When you use this defense strategy against these dragons of demise and distraction, your victory is far more than increased productivity:

You get more time to worship Jesus and focus on your relationship with Him because you have done the necessary prep-work to have this vital time already allocated in to your schedule. You get more time to read your Bible and pray, every single morning because you have already slayed your dragons and can have an epic time of reading about the Greater Dragon Slayer: Jesus Christ. You get to achieve more of your goals and be much closer to the dreams that God has placed into your mind for you to accomplish by His grace, for His glory and for the joy of the people in your life.

Chapter 18

START SIMPLE

making the best use of the time, because the days are evil.
(Eph. 5:16)

"If you don't manage your time, time will eventually manage you."

CA few years back, I was enrolled in seminary full-time, working a full-time job and involved in a local church, full time. At the same time, I was adjusting to a brand new state and a brand new environment. Above all that, I was newly married. I do believe though, at least for men, that they are impressively more intentional with a heavy load on their shoulders. The weight of responsibility carries with it a realization that we are not able to accomplish everything ourselves—and this in turn perpetuates us to press in to Christ more and more.

I love figuring out life hacks that catapult my productivity beyond my wildest imagination. When I learn to do something more efficiently and expediently—I get frustrated that I did not learn it earlier. This is why I write this, to help you avoid that frustration. Here is the shockingly simple thing that I started doing that not only increased my productivity—but deepened the clarity I experience—in every single sphere of my life:

I intentionally choose to exclusively focus on one task and have entirely quit believing in the multi-tasking myth.

This takes deliberate intentionality—because of all the things in your life that are aggressively pursuing your attention. You should be the wise manager of your life and all the urgent items should not be managing you.

One of the biggest distractions that we face which deplete our clarity and often stifle our creativity is technology. I know, big surprise here. So instead of technology managing you, administer technology in a way in which you are the manager of it.

Here are four shockingly simple tips that I am confident will dramatically increase your productivity:

1. **Repent From Believing In The Multi-Tasking Myth.** Focus on one task at a time. It does not matter what the task is. Do just that task. If I am writing a new book—all I have open is a word-processing program. That is it. I only use my Chrome browser if I need to research something. Why be so rigorous about such scheduling you ask? Because

every time we switch to a different task or we dive into the multi-tasking myth, we lose the momentum that we have gained. The crazy thing is that this has a direct effect on our heart. A study was done indicating that those who were not constantly checking their email felt more able to do their job and stay on task. It took some of them five days to have a more natural, variable heart-rate. Being still and knowing God is in control has never been more relevant or pertinent than in the digital media age in which we are living in.

2. **Quit Being Notified To Death.** Check notifications at specifically scheduled time blocks during your day. Morning, afternoon and late evening is what works best for me. Based on your job, activity and life-style, another type of schedule will be better. Find what works for you and stick to it. I have completely shut off push-button notifications on every one of my devices and apps. This means that I check notifications when the allotted time in my schedule allows for it. I check my email three times a day. In the morning, to see if anything urgent came in over-night. In the afternoon and again a bit later in the evening. I use the same method for all social media, responding to Facebook comments, Twitter activity and blog comments. Set up a deliberate time limit and do not go into over-time. This has dramatically increased the clarity that I experience in my life. If you can't overcome the temptation of checking notifications while reading your Bible app, go ahead and switch to a paper Bible.

3. **Do Not Disturb.** I love the *"do not disturb"* feature on the iPhone. Set it up so that you are not distracted by any

new notifications. This is especially helpful when you are reading your Bible, creating new content, practicing your art or craft or just working in general.

4. **Forget Finding The Perfect Time.** Often, we do not perfect an art or a skill we have because we are always looking for the right time or the perfect atmosphere. You will never find it. If you have a spare thirty minutes, write that next paragraph that you want people to read. Edit whatever it is that you are working on. Gradual progress is better than perfect procrastination.

I love the concept of stewardship and how it is presented to is in the Bible. It is required of stewards that they be found faithful. If someone was to conduct an internal audit, assessing the level of faithfulness, in your use of time given to you by God, day by day, would you pass flawlessly or would there be many areas of concern, in need of correction?

More than that, we are not just managers and stewards of our stuff or our schedule, we are servants of Christ and stewards of the mysteries of God. This is a great privilege and an immense responsibility (1. Cor. 4:1-2). As we seek to display Jesus to the watching world, we do well to start doing shockingly simple things that increase our effectivity, while here on earth.

Chapter 19

GENERATE AWESOME

Whatever you do, work heartily, as
for the Lord and not for men
(Col. 3:23)

*"Some of us don't need a better job, we just
need to do the job we have better."*

I will never forget what one disgruntled barista told me upon taking my order. I asked him if he was having a good time while working. He looked at me like I just ordered an iced venti, ristretto shot, hazelnut Americano with two inches of breve. *Good time?* he stammered—*no way. The only time I enjoy life is when I am on the opposite side of this counter*—was the lackluster reply. Luckily, my drink came out ok and I was on my way.

There are three basic things that people at work think about all day long:

What time is my break.
What time is my lunch.
What time am I off.

I believe that these three are killers of any creativity that may have otherwise been displayed. Why does this happen? At what point did our brains get re-wired into thinking that when we step in to work, the passion, the joy and the creativity are left sitting in the back seat of our car waiting to be re-united with us during our next ten minute break.

You and I were created by a Creator God who made us to be creative human beings. Work is not a curse but rather a blessing. When we do the work well and flourish in our current environment, we image Jesus to the watching world. Why? Because everything we do is a reflection of what Jesus did to us. We work as unto the Lord because the Lord provided us with *the* work (Col. 3: 23-24).

When Jesus created the world, He had dirt under His fingernails. He tended the garden. Jesus is the Great Gardener (Gen. 3:8). So when you and I work and we do our work well, we are displaying the Greatest Worker to the watching world.

Here are ten things you can start doing right now to move forward with your current job:

1. **Be awesome, even if your employer is not.** What specifically can you bring to your current environment to enhance it. How can you use your God-given abilities to radically change the ambiance of the work environment that is less than awesome?

2. **Less excuses, more solutions.** I really do believe that some employees go into a state of euphoria when they say *no* to a request from a customer. I recently came in to a cell phone store. Before I was even able to form a complete sentence, I was told a definitive *no*, three times. Find a way to say *yes*, more often.

3. **Embrace scarcity.** Instead of focusing on the resources you do not have, creatively use what you do have and see how you can excel. Very often, a lack of resources is actually a catalyst that propels your creativity into a sphere where it would otherwise not go.

4. **Forget about the clock.** If you want to do work that matters, it will require of you emotional labor. Quit worrying about when *your* break is coming up and focus on the people in front of you who *need* a break—and you are there to help them.

5. **Be faithful in little.** I firmly believe in the principle that *"he who is faithful in little is also faithful in much"* (Luke 16:10). If you are a good steward with what you have been given, you will eventually be given more. I remember when I worked in a small cubicle, making one hundred calls every hour, interrupting people as they sat down for dinner. Half

a decade later, I was sitting in a corner office, with carpet on the floor, not on the wall. In both environments, my principle was simple: Do the best possible job that you can, in the environment that you are in. Excel in generating awesome, everywhere.

6. **Stop living in the future and start living in the present.** What would happen if you approached your day job as if it were your dream job. How would that change the quality of the work that you do?

7. **Be amazing, even if your job is not.** What if you stopped worrying about when you are *off* and started intentionally being *on*, all the time? Even if it was boring. Even if there was not an instant reward. Even if no one was watching. Even if you were not going to get an engraved award which would turn into a useless paper-weight, moments after you receive it?

8. **Work on your dream job, at your current job.** No, I do not mean steal from your employer by applying at other places, on companies' time and dime. Here is what I do mean: When I was dialing for days, in my office which was small enough for a family of hamsters to comfortably live in, there was a script. Everyone *read* off the script. I *memorized* the script. I said the same thing, so many times that I eventually did not need a script. I worked on my voice inflection. I changed the way I delivered the pitch. I put my personality in it. I learned how to adjust the speed and emotion of my voice. Pretty soon, people did not mind skipping their dinner and were glad to give me twenty

minutes of their time. This was before I knew that most likely, for the rest of my life I would end up doing two things: speaking and writing.

9. **Create exciting out of the ordinary.** Whatever your dream job may be, use what you are doing now towards your advantage and weave it in to the every day fabric of your current vocation. Why would you allow eight hours a day, to go to waste. Pretty soon, you won't want to take a break, and will work straight through lunch.

10. **Be the change agent.** Be the one to embrace change. Champion a phenomenal attitude. Conquer people with your love. Intentionally remain pleasant to work with. Forget about you and lose yourself in serving other people. Because when you realize it is not about you, this is going to be the best thing that has happened to you.

When we look at our job not as a daily grind but as an opportunity for creativity to be unleashed, our entire perspective experiences a shift. We do not **have** to go to work. We **get** to *go to work*. Do the work. Give Jesus the glory. Spread joy to the people who you work with. Be satisfied in life. Let Jesus take care of your future success. Generate amazing.

Chapter 20

BE PERSISTENT

And whatever you ask in prayer, you
will receive, if you have faith
(Matt. 21:22)

"If you are not reaching your goals, someone else is."

I believe that most people in life do not get where they want
to go because they lack consistency in being persistent. It
is sometimes more fun to talk about an achievement you desire
instead of putting in the effort to create reality out of fantasy.

One of my most memorable parables from Jesus is found in the
gospel according to Luke. It is precisely in this account that
the principle of being persistent is talked about. The skilled
physician explains that persistent prayer is synonymous with an
individual who is captured by Jesus. It almost seems to good

to be true that Jesus is so attentive to our needs. All He asks is for our consistency. He desires to lavish upon us His grace and favor.

I will never forget my first real promotion. I was eighteen years old at the time. I was working for a market research company. We made calls to individuals and conducted surveys for our clients. The job was a pretty good gig. Most people working there were young. We got a five-minute break every hour on the hour. There was an inexpensive vending machine in the break room. Hot chocolate was on the house.

The "*floor*" as it was called, consisted of sixty cubicles. The tiny carpeted cubicle could have been more lavish. Above the *floor* was a large glass office. In this office sat the supervisors. Their job was to monitor the calls being made. To make sure no one falsified information while doing the surveys. Incentives were given out commensurate to the amount of surveys the interviewers completed during their shift.

From the first day that I stepped into this establishment, I was already eyeing the looming glass office. I did not see a reason why I could not be the one monitoring the employees and coaching on how to improve the quality of the call. I already knew that it would be a lot more fun to be in the fishbowl, looking over the small empire. I quickly began to meet the staff and found out who is who. As my success increased in interviewing people about various items, I realized that it was time. It was time to leave the carpeted cubicle and get into the glass office.

After about one month of working on the *floor,* **I began to periodically visit the office of the person who pulled the trigger on all the hiring decisions.** The first time I asked to get the supervisor position, she looked at me in disbelief. *Did you not just start about a month or two ago* she asked a bit annoyed. I said *yes* but you can check my stats and they are well above most veterans on the floor. She asked me to come back later. I continued to knock on her office door on a consistent basis. This season was coupled with persistent prayer.

Then it finally happened. My persistent prayer finally paid off. After submitting an official resume, I was promoted to being a supervisor. Being in the glass office was much more fun. Just as I assumed when I entered the carpeted cubicle, six months ago.

Should you use persistent prayer to get a better position at work? Maybe. Above that, you should pray to experience the fullness of who God is. In the context of our information-saturated world, we have to fight for our right to pray.

So in Luke 18:1-8 we find the parable of the persistent widow. She was adamant about getting the justice that she deserved. **The premise of this parable is for us to always pray and not lose heart.** She kept coming to the judge. He kept refusing to hear her out. Then here is what happened. He finally got fed up with her constantly coming to him. He said that he *neither fears God nor is a respecter of men.* But, because this widow kept bother him—he will give her justice. Jesus continues the parable by explaining it. He is comparing an unrighteous judge who grants something to someone whom he does not like to a righteous God who gives justice to His elect. Jesus is the one who wants to grant you the desires of your heart you see. Jesus said "*He will give justice to them speedily.*"

I love the way Jesus reminds us here of how important our close communion *with* Him is *to* Him. He says that God will give justice to those "*who cry to him day and night.*" Being persistent is a biblical principle. Do not settle for where you are at right now. Jesus has prepared something for you that is far greater than your imagination.

Jesus says: ask and it will be given to you.
Jesus says: knock and it will be opened to you.
Jesus says: everyone who asks receives.
Jesus says: the one who seeks, finds.
Jesus says: the one who knocks, it will be opened.

What He specifically wants from you and me is a perpetual, persistent and passionate prayer life!

I believe that we rarely experience the grandiose presence of God because we are mediocre in our persistence and lackluster in our prayer life. But even with all of this said, there is a temptation to be more satisfied in the gift rather than the giver. We must want Jesus more than what comes from him.

Jesus finishes the parable with a question: He asks: "N*evertheless, when the Son of Man comes, will he find faith on earth?*" Jesus poses this statement as a question. What He is actually doing is encouraging you and I today to be constant and persistent in our prayer. It pleases Jesus when we are praying and communing with him throughout our day.

Do not be afraid to pray audacious prayers—prayers that are absolutely impossible from a human point of view. But with Jesus, nothing is impossible!

GOING FORWARD

*T*hank you for reading this book. My hope is that it helped you in some small way. To dream big. To live life, wide awake. To love Jesus and His gospel. To go forward with your life, in order to make an impact in your life. God wants to lead us to places we have never been before, so that we can learn to trust Him in ways we never have before.

For me, writing is a highly calming exercise where I can take the millions of ideas, buzzing around in my brain and actually put them out into the public arena. If you benefited from anything that I write, then it is just an added bonus to something that I already love doing, probably more than most other things in life.

My goal as a pastor, writer and speaker is to provide amazing content to you, as the reader or listener. I believe in the power of words. I believe words and ideas can and will change the world. God chose words as the primary way to reveal Himself to us. Jesus was the Word that became flesh and dwelt among us, full of grace, glory and truth.

But writing and creating content can be a pretty daunting process.

The scariest part about writing and creating, is that every time you start a new project, you begin at zero. Zero can be pretty intimidating. There is a cursor blinking back at you, on a screen that is completely blank, with no content. It is similar to beginning to write a brand new sermon. You have your Bible, your collection of pens, your trusty journal, Jesus and the Holy Spirit. It's go time. Half the work is done, once you actually start.

But here is the thing: No single creative process can be sustained. You have to keep on creating new content. You can't just write or do your craft for fame or praise or recognition or accolades. Because all of that is great, but it is not enough to sustain your energy and stamina to continue forward. It evaporates quickly and only gives you a short burst of energy.

Whatever art or craft you do, there must be something more that motivates you than success or fame or recognition or money. Because those are poor substitutes for real motivation. So no matter how much the metrics blew up on that last project, I have to get up and put in the hours the next day. And so do you.

Don't live by breathing in fumes of past success. Don't wait for recognition that you might receive in the future. Do what you love and love what you do, right now, in this moment—it is a gift—that is why it is called the *present*.

At the end of the day, it is not about writing but about the Great Writer, who has already written the greatest Script known in human history—the narrative of my life and your life. And once we realize what that is and begin to realize that Jesus is the Hero and not us—this liberates us to do the work that we were created to do—for the benefit of the people in our lives.

I want to thank you personally for reading. Your readership is truly an encouragement to me. I hope that the content you consumed in this book, has served you well. If this book helped you realize that Jesus is your only hope, you are in a good place. We need to supernaturally understand that every problem we have encountered in this world was the result of sin. But there is hope and healing. Every solution to the problems in this world is Jesus. God wants to save you, so that He can love you, forever.

At the conclusion of this book, as we proceed *forward*, I want to leave you with a prayer that was proclaimed by the Apostle Paul. He prayed this over the people that he dearly loved. This is exactly what I want to do as well. I may not know you personally, but I want to pray for you specifically:

I bow my knees before the Father, from whom every family in heaven and on earth is named, that according to the riches of his glory he may grant you to be strengthened with power through his Spirit in your inner being, so that Christ may dwell in your hearts through faith—that you, being rooted and grounded in love, may have strength to comprehend with all the saints what is the breadth and length and height and depth, and to know the love of Christ that surpasses knowledge, that you may be filled with all the fullness of God. Now to him who is able to do far more abundantly than all that we ask or think, according to the power at work within us, to him be glory in the church and in Christ Jesus throughout all generations, forever and ever. Amen. (Eph. 3:14-21).

I wish you an unlimited amount of grace and peace in Christ my friend. May you continue to glorify God and enjoy Him forever.

Bogdan Kipko
Orange County, California
December 2013

CONNECT WITH ME

I would be delighted to connect with you! I certainly don't want for this book to be the only interaction that we ever have. Please connect with me using any or all of the social mediums listed below:

Blog: www.kipko.net
Twitter: www.twitter.com/bogdankipko
Facebook: www.facebook.com/bogdankipko
Instagram: www.instagram.com/kipko
Book Site: www.forwardbook.com
Email: bogdan@bogdankipko.com
iTunes: The Fuel For Life Podcast

CONTINUE THE CONVERSATION

*I*f this book helped you move *forward*, the greatest thing you can do is to tell others about it.

Thank you in advance for spreading the message of the book using any and all of the methods below:

Amazon: Write and post an honest review of the book directly to the book page on Amazon. I just want people to see how this book helped and impacted your life.

Twitter: Tweet and re-tweet as many quotes as you would like from the book, using the following hashtag: #forwardbook

Facebook: Post as many quotes as you would like from the book, using the following hashtag: #forwardbook

Instagram: Upload images with quotes using the following hashtag: #forwardbook

Email me: bogdan (at) bogdankipko.com and let me know how this book helped you move forward with your life. I want to read and reply to your story and celebrate what Jesus is doing in your life.

ACKNOWLEDGMENTS

A book is never a solo project of a lone writer, even if he does spend most of his time writing alone. So many people have helped shape and mold me into who I am today. I am forever grateful to you. I would like to especially thank the following:

- My Lord and Savior, Jesus Christ—even though I have failed miserably, you still saved me gloriously.

- My Wife Victoria—thank you for being beautiful, amazing, supportive and supremely attentive while listening to all of my ideas, thoughts and dreams, this is our journey together!

- My Mom—thank you for praying for me probably more consistently than anyone I know.

- My Community Group—you guys make it an absolute pleasure to teach the Bible to you. Thank you for being such an amazing group who loves Jesus and His Word.

- My Church—thank you for believing in me and sticking with me. Jesus has amazing plans for The Slavic Church. Get ready for the harvest.

- Thank you to my friends, critics, coaches and every person who has ever reached out to encourage me and let me know that content written by me has helped you in some small way. You are the reason I want to continue moving *forward* and keep providing consistently solid content for your good and to serve you well.

ABOUT THE AUTHOR

*B*OGDAN KIPKO is the Lead Visionary at Intentional Christianity, a digital portal dedicated to spreading the supremacy of Jesus Christ to a world in need of radical redemption. He is also a husband, pastor and author who is passionate about cultivating a culture where Jesus is worshiped perpetually and the Bible is exposited faithfully. Bogdan holds a Master's degree in Theology and has studied at The Masters Seminary in Sun Valley, California, and Talbot Theological Seminary in La Mirada, California.

Utilizing timely social mediums such as Twitter, Facebook and his blog, Bogdan is determined to proclaim the timeless message of the gospel to a generation seeking hope and healing, which only Jesus can provide. For more information, please visit www.kipko.net.

Bogdan and his wife Victoria currently live in Southern California.